FOUNDATIONS OF MODERN HISTORY

General Editor A. Goodwin

Professor of Modern History, The University of Manchester

In the FOUNDATIONS OF MODERN HISTORY *Series*

Further titles to be announced.

25954
973.311
Chr

FOUNDATIONS OF MODERN HISTORY

Crisis of Empire

Great Britain and the American Colonies
1754-1783

by I. R. CHRISTIE

Professor of History,
University College,
The University of London

W · W · NORTON & COMPANY

New York · London

Schuylerville Public Library

COPYRIGHT © 1966 BY I. R. CHRISTIE
Library of Congress Catalog Card No. 66-28649

W. W. Norton & Company, Inc., 500 Fifth Avenue, New York, N.Y. 10110
W. W. Norton & Company Ltd., 37 Great Russell Street, London WC1B 3NU

SBN 393-09650-5
PRINTED IN THE UNITED STATES OF AMERICA
3 4 5 6 7 8 9 0

General Preface

THIS series of short historical studies has as its main theme successive phases in the evolution of modern history from Renaissance times to the present day. Its general purpose is to provide within a limited compass, and at a reasonable cost, scholarly surveys of some of the fundamental developments which have influenced the civilization and conditioned the outlook of the modern world. A second aim of the series will be to illustrate how not only the general direction of recent historical inquiry but also its very content and its relations with other disciplines have been progressively modified. If students of scientific or technological subjects who are extending their interests to the 'liberal' arts or social sciences are made aware of these trends something will have been done to close the gap between the scientific and human cultures. A further feature of the series will be the endeavour to present selected periods of British history against the contemporary background of European development, with special emphasis on the nature and extent of cultural, scientific or intellectual interchange. Here the object will be to demonstrate the unity as well as the diversity of the European heritage and to re-examine its evolving significance in the context of global history.

In this volume Mr. Christie reconsiders the eighteenth-century crisis in the British government's relations with its North American colonies which resulted in the independence of the United States of America. He studies this decisive turning point in world history primarily from the point of view of the British ministers who were charged with the responsibility of re-designing the whole administrative and military structure of Imperial government after the Seven Years War. He brings to this task his own special knowledge of British political life in the reign of George III and is thus able to explain how and why Grenville's ministry came to apply to the American colonies those policies which have too often been depicted as novel, irrational and oppressive. Mr. Christie demonstrates that these policies were by no means wholly new, that they were in essence reasonable, coherent and, in the circumstances of the time, defensible. Their timing proved, in the event, to have been unfortunate, but their real flaw was that they failed to provide the essential basis of colonial assent. In his analysis of the subsequent disputes with the colonial assemblies the author shows why the conciliatory Rockingham administration, while repealing the obnoxious Stamp Act, was obliged by the exigencies of the Parliamentary situation at Westminster to introduce a Declaratory Act which, though intentionally ambiguous in its wording, made the British insistence on Parliamentary supremacy the touchstone of the constitutional conflict.

The real failure of British statesmanship is thus seen to lie, less in the policies of the Grenville ministry, than in the inept and obstinate attempt of Charles Townshend in 1767 to raise a revenue in America from customs duties and to apply part of the proceeds to ensure the financial independence of the colonial governors, judges and officials. These measures convinced the Americans that the British government was determined to undermine the constitutional privileges of the colonial assemblies and steeled their resistance to Lord North's subsequent policies of coercion. Mr. Christie's conclusion is that the loss of the American colonies was also attributable to the mistaken fears of the colonists that they were in danger of being reduced to the level of slaves and to the equally unjustified British conviction that American independence would involve the mother country's loss of great power status. Ironically, independence posed problems for the emancipated American states which nearly led to civil strife among themselves at a time when a new and more vigorous British empire was already rising from the ashes of the old.

Contents

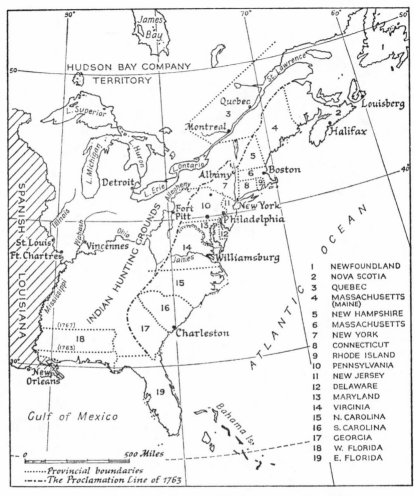

1	NEWFOUNDLAND
2	NOVA SCOTIA
3	QUEBEC
4	MASSACHUSETTS (MAINE)
5	NEW HAMPSHIRE
6	MASSACHUSETTS
7	NEW YORK
8	CONNECTICUT
9	RHODE ISLAND
10	PENNSYLVANIA
11	NEW JERSEY
12	DELAWARE
13	MARYLAND
14	VIRGINIA
15	N. CAROLINA
16	S. CAROLINA
17	GEORGIA
18	W. FLORIDA
19	E. FLORIDA

.... Provincial boundaries
— · — · — The Proclamation Line of 1763

Eastern America 1763

Introduction

THE American Revolution was one of the decisive events in modern history – not merely in the history of western civilization but of the world. As a result of the developments outlined in this book, the greater part of the British Empire in the New World became an independent nation, still intimately linked by trade with Britain and with Europe, but for over a century politically withdrawn from both. A new and enriching diversity was established in the human quest of knowledge and experience of that all-important art, political organization. Henceforth the British commitment to representative government and the rule of law pursued not one but two lines of development: on the one hand, towards British parliamentary democracy; on the other, towards the American brand of democracy within a federal mould, incorporating written constitutions, a separation of powers, and judicial review. The intellectual interplay between two great systems, akin but separate, could strengthen and stimulate them both. More immediately, the American struggle for independence precipitated the chain reaction in Europe associated with the French Revolution and Napoleon. By the successful American appeal to it, a new cachet was given to the liberal trend in eighteenth-century European political thought; and it was the fiscal bankruptcy which participation in the American war brought upon the government of France that led to the convening of the States-General in 1789, with all its consequences for France, for Europe, and for the world. How momentous the American Revolution may have been in other ways can only be a matter of speculation. The nineteenth century was the century of British ascendancy. What mark might the two branches of the English-speaking peoples have left upon it, had they remained united within one empire or commonwealth? And what might have been the consequences, had the old régimes in France and other parts of Europe crumbled less catastrophically and not in the context of revolution in America?

During the last sixty or seventy years historical inquiry has

1

broadened and deepened to a tremendous extent our knowledge and understanding of the events which led to the breakdown of the first British Empire and the emergence as an
independent power of the United States. Through the efforts
of a host of scholars, a vast range of original correspondence
and documentation has been gradually made available in
print and numerous monographs have contributed to the
elucidation of this significant episode in the story of modern
western civilization. During the process there has inevitably
been some shifting of interpretations, and the reader will find
some brief guidance about this in chapter VII. Fuller accounts
will be found in Michael Kraus, *The Writing of American
History* (Norman, Okl., 1953), and in the first two chapters of
H. Hale Bellot, *American History and American Historians* (1952).
This book is an attempt to present a straightforward narrative
of events in the light of the more recent conclusions of the
specialists. The general reader who wishes to explore the
subject in more detail will find further guidance in the Bibliography.

It remains for me to thank those who have helped me with
the making of this book. Mr. D. H. Watson made available
his expert knowledge on Rockingham's relations with the
merchants and saved me from some errors of fact in chapter
IV. Mr. John Ehrman kindly read through the whole of the
typescript. I am very grateful to them both for their advice,
and also to Mrs. K. Munro, who typed the final draft.

December 1965   IAN R. CHRISTIE

CHAPTER ONE

North Atlantic Empire

ABOUT 1750 the British Empire in America comprised eight
island colonies in the Atlantic and Caribbean – Jamaica; the
Leeward Islands, Antigua, Nevis, St. Kitts, and Montserrat;
Barbados, Bermuda, and the Bahamas – and fifteen provinces
stretched along the eighteen hundred or so miles of the
American eastern seaboard: Newfoundland, Nova Scotia,
Massachusetts (including present-day Maine), New Hamp-
shire, Rhode Island, Connecticut, New York, New Jersey,
Pennsylvania with Delaware, Maryland, Virginia, North and
South Carolina, and Georgia.

In Newfoundland a few thousand settlers were clustered
round St. Johns and Placentia on the Avalon peninsula and
only the most rudimentary elements of civil administration had
yet been established. Nova Scotia, taken from the French in
1713, inhabited by some ten thousand settlers of French
descent, most of whom were shortly afterwards (1755) to be
expelled, was little more than a military outpost. The remaining thirteen provinces, all subsequently to be involved
in the American Revolution, had a total population roughly
estimated at about one and a quarter million (excluding a
further two hundred thousand Negro slaves, more than half
of whom were concentrated in the coastal areas of Virginia).*

Everywhere from New England to the Carolinas, the
flow of settlement had long surged across the tide-water to

* The following approximate estimates are derived from Lawrence Henry
Gipson, *The British Empire before the American Revolution* (New York, 1936–65),
vols. II and III: Massachusetts with Maine, 220,000; New Hampshire,
25,000; Rhode Island, 40,000; Connecticut, 125,000; New York, 95,000;
New Jersey, 65,000; Pennslyvania, with Delaware, 250,000; Maryland,
whites, 150,000, blacks, 40,000; Virginia, whites, 170,000, blacks, 120,000;
N. Carolina, whites, 60,000, blacks, 15,000; S. Carolina, whites, 25,000,
blacks, 39,000; Georgia, less than 5,000. On colonial population figures see
E. B. Greene and V. D. Harrington, *American population figures before the
Federal Census of 1790* (N.Y., 1932).

distances varying from a hundred and fifty to more than two hundred miles inland. At many points it lapped the eastern flanks of the Appalachian range which divides the coastal plains from the river systems of the interior; and in western Virginia a trickle of settlers had crossed the watershed into the valleys of the New and Greenbriar rivers. Most purely English in stock were the populations of the New England provinces, Massachusetts, New Hampshire, Rhode Island, and Connecticut. Further west and south there were significant admixtures of other strains. In New York, wrested from the United Provinces in the mid-seventeenth century, the Dutch element remained strong. From early in the eighteenth century there was a large-scale spontaneous migration of Ulster Scots into northern New Jersey, and during the same period considerable numbers were brought to Pennsylvania as indentured servants. Restless individualists, well suited to frontier life, they soon drifted southwards in considerable numbers, following the line of the uplands, to people the back country of Virginia and the Carolinas. Germans, many of them seeking escape from religious persecution, settled in large numbers in Pennsylvania, Maryland, Virginia and the Carolinas. Highly valued as workers, they were eagerly sought by employers wanting hands and by colonial authorities anxious to people frontier districts: one contemporary estimated in 1755 that half the population of Pennsylvania was of German extraction. The British government welcomed this foreign influx, feeling a need to husband the human resources of the home country. The only British migration which it encouraged was that of socially undesirable elements. Large numbers were sent out after criminal conviction to indentured service, usually for a seven-year term, and most of them, after working out their sentences, remained in America, where economic opportunities were far greater for the vigorous individualist than they were at home.

Along much of the inland frontier of settlement, from New York to Georgia, British settlers were in frequent contact with the Indian peoples of the interior, and individual traders had occasionally penetrated westwards for hundreds of miles into the wilderness. A profitable traffic was carried on, the Indians selling furs in exchange for muskets, gunpowder, rum, cloth, brass cooking kettles, hatchets, knives and other metalware.

By the 'forties competition with the French was reaching a critical stage. The French, pushing forward from their bases in Canada established nearly thirty trading posts in the area of the Great Lakes, while others belonging to the French colony of Louisiana were set up in the Illinois country south of Lake Michigan, notably at Fort Chartres, on the upper Mississippi and at Fort Vincennes on the Wabash river. In trade the British had certain distinct advantages. Except for the New Yorkers at Albany, whose reputation was bad, they were more open in their dealings with the Indians, paid more generously for the furs they took, and could offer a better range of trade goods at lower prices and in more abundance. On the other hand the British were colonisers, which the French, present in far small numbers in the New World, did not appear to be. On the borders of settled New York the land hunger of speculators pressed upon the hunting grounds of the Six Nations in the upper Mohawk valley. Pennsylvanians were feeling their way towards exploitation of the lands in the valley of the Allegheny. In Virginia a score or more of land companies had come into existence with extensive and competing designs for enormous concessions in the Ohio valley. The Indian's attitude to the European was ambivalent. On the one hand, he had become so accustomed to hunting with firearms, and to the use and enjoyment of other western manufactures, that a return to a more primitive but independent kind of life had become impossible. On the other, he feared the European as a settler and was therefore inclined to favour the French, who seemed in this respect less dangerous. By 1750 Indian resistance to any further British westward movement was stiffening. During the next year or so the French, unable to beat the British out of the Indian trade by other means, and concerned about the threat of large-scale settlement under the auspices of the Virginian Ohio company, resolved upon military occupation and annexation of the upper Ohio valley and were able to exploit to this end the Indian concern for their hunting grounds. As the Virginians were prepared to fight for their claims, an armed clash for control of the interior became imminent.

Economically the Empire was much diversified. Almost everywhere, except in the coastal regions from the Chesapeake southwards, a large proportion of the colonists were engaged,

as tenants or independent cultivators, in general farming, and
most of the mainland colonies provided a surplus of agricultural produce for export. But this apart, the economy of each
region had distinctive characteristics. In New England, particularly Massachusetts, capital and labour were channelled
into navigation, fishing, and ship-building. Boston, the commercial metropolis of the British possessions in North America,
was the greatest trading and shipping centre in the Empire
outside the British Isles. Its ships and its seamen played a vital
part in maintaining the network of ocean trade routes which
sustained the Empire. Similar in character was Rhode Island,
the chief colonial participant in the slave trade. Boston and
Rhode Island, and to a lesser extent New York, were the main
centres of the flourishing rum distilling industry. About 1750
there were no less than 63 distilleries in Massachusetts and
little short of two million gallons a year were exported from
the colony, much of it as essential trade-stores for the fur
trade in the interior and for the slave traffic of the West
African coast. New Hampshire's chief wealth lay in its forests,
sources of masts and ship-timber, though the more accessible
regions were becoming denuded of the great white pine trees
prized as mainmasts for king's ships. New York province,
owing to restrictive land policies in the past, was relatively less
developed, and the potentialities of a native iron industry were
not yet realized; Albany, inland up the Hudson, was a centre
for a profitable Indian fur trade. In Pennsylvania an extensive
iron industry had come into existence, capable of supplying
an increasing share of the Empire's needs in axes, knives,
scythes, nails, and various other kinds of metalware – a phe-
nomenon causing intense disquiet to competing interests in
Great Britain. The capital, Philadelphia, while not to be
compared for commercial importance with Boston, was at this
time perhaps the most populous town in the British settlements, had a small ship-building industry, and was an important centre for the fur trade.

All these colonies shared the characteristic of being suffi-
ciently similar to Great Britain in climate and natural resources
to tend rather to compete with than to complement the
British economy. It was otherwise with the colonies to the
southward. The tide-water regions of Maryland and Virginia
favoured the employment of large slave populations in the

ulture of tobacco, their staple export to the home country. So much did this one crop dominate the economy of both these provinces that in the absence of an adequate metal currency it was commonly used as a medium of exchange. Further south still the economy of the two Carolinas showed general similarities, though neither had reached a comparable stage of economic or social progress. Some tobacco was grown in North Carolina. The sandy 'pine-barrens', inland of the tide-water, too poor to serve other purposes, had made it foremost in the Empire for the production of various naval stores – tar, pitch, resin, and turpentine. In its southerly coastal districts, as in South Carolina, the staple crop was rice, of which great quantities were shipped from both provinces to Great Britain, mostly for re-export to northern Europe. In South Carolina, too, the culture of indigo was found profitable, and a limited but lucrative trade for deerskins was carried on with the Indians. Georgia as yet was little more than a frontier post against the Spanish in Florida. Founded in 1732, its economic development was retarded by the ban on slavery imposed by the trustees of the corporation and quickened only after the lapse in 1752, of their charter and the abandonment of their policies.

The economies of the island colonies were wholly dependent upon their staple crop of sugar. Though sugar planting was still just profitable, the islands were running into considerable difficulties. The assured market in Britain was virtually saturated, and neither the planters nor the sugar traders and refiners in London and Bristol were able to expand into the continental market in face of superior French competition. For this a combination of factors was responsible. Less burdened by taxation the French planters were better cultivators, and the soils of their islands were better, whereas that of the British island plantations was poor and also exhausted by over-cropping. Longer established, the British sugar-growing industry also carried a far higher burden of debt. The British islands (and also the French) were almost wholly dependent on external sources of provisions and timber as well as other requirements of civilized living. In these adverse circumstances the concern of all those various groups engaged in any way in the sugar trade to save and profit from their investments was a recurring factor in imperial politics.

Almost from its beginnings, and particularly during the last hundred years, economic development within the Empire had been to some extent consciously shaped by government action, following certain preoccupations and preconceptions which came to harden into principle. The resulting system is sometimes described as mercantilist. It is perhaps more straightforward to think of it simply as protectionist, with the object of making the Empire strong and economically and militarily self-sustained in a world of similar competing systems, among which that of the French seemed especially formidable.

Prior among the requirements of such a system was sea power, a first line of defence against invasion of the metropolis and an essential safeguard of the trade routes across the oceans. By a series of Navigation and Trade Acts, from 1660 onwards, foreign ships were barred from the ports of British colonies and a monopoly of the intra-imperial carrying trade was established for British and colonial shipping. No foreign imperialism was to creep in under the cloak of trade, the transport facilities of the Empire would be well served and in reliable hands, and in time of war the navy would have an ample source of seamen for impressment.

Secondly these Acts were designed to make Great Britain the entrepôt for colonial trade. This policy satisfied various requirements. It insured that Great Britain obtained first call on various colonial staples and might be in a position to deny them to competitors. It assured freedom from dependence upon sources under foreign control. It brought British merchants a share of profit on the re-export trade, particularly in such commodities as tobacco and rice. It enabled the British government to levy customs duties (though most of these were refunded on goods which were re-exported) and to secure various other contributions in the form of harbour and shipping dues. In pursuit of this policy the Acts prohibited the export direct to foreign countries of various staple commodities produced in the colonies. From 1660 sugar, tobacco, cotton-wool, indigo, ginger, and other dyestuffs were on the enumerated list. These enumerated commodities, at first, apart from tobacco, mainly the products of the island colonies, later came to include more and more of the exports from the American mainland: rice, molasses, and rum, were added in

1704; naval stores of all kinds in 1705; copper, and beaver and other furs in 1721. But considerable ranges of colonial produce were left untouched by these regulations. The British at home had no commercial interest in agricultural produce or in furniture, casks, and the innumerable other articles made from timber, and the colonists were free to carry these to any market to which they might be admitted.

It is by no means simple to assess the balance of advantage or disadvantage to the colonists from this system.* The British commercial metropolis certainly levied its toll; but it is by no means clear that, had Britain not been made the entrepôt for the colonial trade, any resulting profit would have gone into the pockets of the colonists rather than into those of European competitors. And in return for these restrictions the colonists were conceded a monopoly on the British market for their staple products, competing foreign sugar and other commodities being discouraged or absolutely excluded by high tariffs. Bounties were granted on certain of their products, notably indigo, naval stores, and ship timber. Behind the shelter of the navigation acts a flourishing ship-building industry had been built up in North America and a great part of the mercantile marine which served the Empire was American owned and American manned.

Lack of foresight made the system work badly at times; but it was directed with a goodwill and an intention to try to balance competing interests. One striking sacrifice was made by the British. During the late seventeenth century a prosperous home tobacco-growing industry in the west Midlands was stamped out in a prolonged and ruthless campaign of law enforcement, in the interests of the Maryland and Virginia planters. Modification was sometimes made in the system of enumerated goods, mainly in order to enable colonists to sell goods at a cheaper rate in southern Europe than would be possible if the price bore the whole cost of shipping through a British port: thus, in the 1730s the southern mainland colonies were successively given the right to ship rice direct to Europe south of Cape Finisterre, and in 1739 this concession was extended to West Indian sugars. On the other hand the home

* See O. M. Dickerson, *The Navigation Acts and the American Revolution* (Phil., London, 1951), for the view that the acts were beneficial to the colonists.

government was concerned to maintain imperial markets for home industries and to protect the most important of these from colonial competition. A Wool Act of 1699 prohibited the export from any colony of raw wool, woollen yarn, or cloth; the Hat Act of 1732 restricted to two the number of apprentices a hatter in the colonies might employ and forebade the export of beaver hats; and the Iron Act of 1750 placed legal prohibitions upon the further expansion of the colonial metalware industry while at the same time attempting, by reductions of import duties, to encourage the shipment of pig and bar iron to Britain – in neither of which objects was it successful.

The most contentious of these commercial adjustments, one which had brought the question of Parliament's power within the Empire under review, the Molasses Act of 1733, did not touch Britain itself but was an attempt to arbitrate between the competing claims of the sugar islands and the New England provinces. Having no native staple products with which to pay for the many essential goods and luxuries imported from Britain, the men of Massachusetts and other northern colonies had developed complex systems of commerce to provide them with the means of payment. Part of the necessary credits they secured from the British West Indies in return for supplies of provisions and timber; but as this market was too limited for their requirements they had extended it to the French West Indies. From these foreign islands came the bulk of the vast quantities of molasses which, turned into rum in the New England distilleries, might be traded for furs for the London market or for West African slaves who might be exchanged for further West Indian products or possibly for silver bullion from the Spanish Main.

British West Indian sugar interests were provoked into threefold complaint: French molasses being cheaper, they themselves were being cut out of a lucrative export trade; their own staple was placed in competition with French sugar refined in New England and then passed off as British on the home market to evade the discriminatory duties; and the sale of indispensable provisions to the French islands was succouring their rivals and was a primary reason for the French success in beating British sugar out of the European market. To these charges the New Englanders replied, that the British islands alone could not supply them with nearly enough molasses to make the rum on which large sections of their commerce were directly or indirectly based, and that without cheap rum their economy would founder.

Walpole's remedy met the islanders' complaint in the letter but did little for them in practice. The Molasses Act imposed heavy duties on foreign sugars, rum and molasses imported into a British colony. Whether this act, if properly enforced, particularly with regard to the article of molasses, would have wreaked the havoc on the New Englanders' economy which they anticipated is open to doubt.* But the situation was dominated by their belief that ruin would ensue; they involved many local customs officials in their determination not to pay what they thought to be a disastrous and iniquitous imposition (though making payments on a lower rate which, in the main, the customs officers seem to have pocketed for themselves); and, whether from complaisance, or from suspicion that a mistake had been made, the home government made no attempt at enforcement. In 1739 it tried to help the sugar planters by giving leave for direct shipment of sugar to southern Europe. But it carefully side-stepped repeated demands from the West Indians, that the New England trade with the French islands should be entirely suppressed.

Under this controlled economy, whatever its shortcomings and the impossibility of completely reconciling all interests, the colonies were in a prosperous state in the mid-eighteenth century. The homes of the commercial aristocracy of New England and of the planters further south were scenes of comfortable, often gracious, living; the financial burden of government was light and the incidence of local taxation negligible or non-existent. Capital was available for economic expansion, some of it from Britain but much within the colonies themselves; and they could even sustain an increase of population of such dimensions that in most of them the numbers were doubling in less than thirty years.

British administrative control over the colonies suffered from a division of responsibility among various departments. Some correspondence was carried on by the secretary of state for the southern department and in time of war the direction of military affairs made his role considerable. Staffs of

* See the discussion of this point, for a period twenty years later, in L. H. Gipson, *The coming of the Revolution 1763–1775* (1954), pp. 62–64.

subordinate boards under the Treasury were responsible for the collection of various royal and imperial revenues in America and, in part, for the enforcement of the laws of trade; and the problems of finance gave the Treasury an important voice at times in the shaping of colonial policy. The Privy Council – operating through appropriate committees, attended by a small group of ministers chiefly concerned with colonial affairs – received petitions, heard appeals from colonial courts, approved commissions and instructions to colonial officials, and disallowed colonial legislation, acting when necessary on recommendations of the appropriate department. This was in most cases the Board of Trade, the agency which, in the eighteenth century, came nearest to acting as a general supervising department, record office, and clearing house for colonial affairs. It conducted a vast correspondence with colonial authorities, received reports, conducted investigations, drafted commissions and instructions, and furnished information and advice for the Privy Council, the executive departments, and Parliament. It provided an important element of continuity in colonial policy; and its recommendations were in general well-digested and judicious, though lacking the balance that might have been achieved had care been taken to include among the commissioners some men with thorough personal experience of American conditions. About 1750, after some years of neglect and inactivity, the Board was coming to the fore under the aggressive leadership of the recently-appointed First Commissioner, the Earl of Halifax, whose object was to turn it into an effective executive department. In 1752 he secured for it the right to appoint the colonial governors and to act as the main channel for their correspondence (powers which were to be lost again by the Board during the 'sixties).

Of the latent conflicts of authority which lurked half-hidden within the constitutional structure of the Empire, none was of more potentially disastrous character than that between Parliament and the colonial legislatures. Attempts have been made to show that parliamentary claims of authority over the colonies were in excess of its historic jurisdiction; but the arguments on the other side are weighty;* and in any case,

* For the case against the claims of Parliament see C. H. McIlwain, *The American Revolution* (London and New York, 1923); and in support

the situation in the eighteenth century was dominated by the conviction of the British political class that Parliament had such powers. In practice Parliament did legislate regularly for the colonies, but mainly in the rather restricted field of imperial trade and navigation. This legislation, notably the Navigation and Trade Acts of 1660, 1661, 1663, 1696, and also numerous later amendments, was on the whole accepted without protest by the colonists, for whom inclusion in the regulated commercial system of the British Empire was in many ways profitable. Hitherto little parliamentary legislation had touched on the domestic affairs of the colonists, though there were a few notable examples: the Wool Act of 1699, the Hat Act of 1732, the Iron Act of 1750. In 1729 Parliament authorized the transfer to the Crown of the rights of the Carolina proprietors when the change from proprietorial to royal government took place, and in the 1730s it sanctioned the expenditure of public money for the founding of Georgia. But the general abstention of Parliament from interference in the domestic concerns of the colonists tended to confirm an assumption, quite contrary to the nascent British concept of parliamentary sovereignty, that domestic legislation was reserved exclusively to their own assemblies.

In the British view, the legislative powers of Parliament included the power to lay taxes. In 1726, forty years before George Grenville's fateful Stamp Act, the imposition of a stamp duty in the colonies by act of Parliament was advocated by a member of the Board of Trade. Veiled threats of such a measure were made on several occasions during the 1720s, in the course of controversies with the assemblies of Massachusetts and of New York over the grant of permanent salaries to the colonial governors. The nearest approach to use of the taxing power before 1764 was in the Molasses Act of 1733. Hairs have been split ever since regarding the fact that, although this act imposed customs duties, it was really an act of controlling trade, not a measure of taxation, 'an act of prohibition not of revenue'.* But the colonists did not see it in

---

* H. E. Egerton, *The Causes and Character of the American Revolution* (1931), p. 71.

of them, R. L. Schuyler, *Parliament and the British Empire* (London and New York, 1929). In the view of the present writer, Schuyler has the better of the argument. His view is the one generally accepted by historians.

this light, and it elicited from them the most outspoken rejection of Parliament's authority to tax them. The agent for Rhode Island protested, that the act was 'divesting them of their rights and privileges as the King's natural-born subjects and Englishmen, in levying subsidies upon them against their consent, when they are annexed to no county in Great Britain, have no representative in Parliament, nor have any part of the legislature of this kingdom.'* Long before the Revolution the principle of 'no taxation without representation' had been clearly proclaimed by the colonists. Nevertheless the fact that the New England merchants were prepared to compound to pay at least a small proportion of the statutory duty on molasses indicated their indifference to the point of principle.†

In the mid-eighteenth century three variations of representative government were established among the American mainland colonies which were later to revolt and form the nucleus of the United States. In all cases the governments originated in grants or acts of the British Crown: during the arguments which preceded the Revolution, there was at least this historical justification for the colonists' final protests that they were subordinate to the Crown but not to Parliament.

Connecticut and Rhode Island were charter colonies. Here the form of government had survived, as established in the mid-seventeenth century, in the shape of a chartered company. The result was an extreme degree of independence. In both colonies the governor, his deputy, the treasurer and secretary, and members of the council were popularly elected each year, and in Rhode Island the assembly also made annual choice of some three hundred subordinate executive and judicial officers, including the judges. The executive governments were thus closely tied to popular wishes, and public affairs were carried on with the minimum of interference from London. Election of deputies to a general assembly took place annually in Connecticut, twice a year in Rhode Island. The legislatures, constituted by assembly, council, and governor, were highly responsive to popular pressure. Owing to the

* Cited in A. B. Keith, *Constitutional History of the First British Empire* (Oxford 1930), p. 337.

† B. Knollenberg, *The origins of the American Revolution, 1759–1766* (N.Y., 1961), pp. 131–2.

extent of the freedoms granted in the charters there was very little that the British government could do to enforce conformity with the rest of the Empire: it could not even sustain the claim to disallow legislation passed in either colony. About mid-century the position of Connecticut was neatly described: 'This government is a sort of republic. They acknowledge the King of Great Britain for sovereign, but are not accountable to the Crown for any acts of government, legislative or administrative.'* It seems probable that, when the imperial crisis developed, the example of these colonies was a stimulus to defiance on the part of less favoured provinces.

After 1752 there were only three proprietary colonies on the American mainland – Maryland, and Pennsylvania with Delaware, Delaware being very closely linked with Pennsylvania, sharing the same governor though having its own assembly. In these colonies the form of government rested partly on the charter granted to the proprietor, under which certain rights were reserved to the Crown, and partly upon the instruments of government issued under the charter by the proprietor. Thus in the charter of privileges granted to Pennsylvania by William Penn in 1701, the government was vested in a governor (the proprietor's deputy) and the freemen, represented in a general assembly elected annually. As the governor's council was created as a purely advisory body, not part of the legislature, Pennsylvania under this constitution had single-chamber representative government. The governor was appointed by the proprietor with the approval of the Crown and acted first and foremost as his agent. Legislation was by Penn, his heirs, and their deputies, with the assent of the freemen acting through the assembly; and in practice the governor frequently withheld consent to bills on instructions from the proprietors. Under the charter there was provision for all legislation to be sent to Britain, where it was subject to royal veto within a period of six months after receipt by the Privy Council. In general this type of government worked rather similarly to the royal government in the remaining colonies, but it caused more friction than occurred in any other province, owing to the

---

* Cited in A. B. Keith, *Constitutional History of the First British Empire* (Oxford, 1930), p. 176; and for a similar judgment twenty years later, *Acts of the Privy Council, Colonial Series*, IV, pp. 445–47.

conflicting claims of inhabitants, proprietor, and the government at home.

With the partial exception of Massachusetts the other mainland colonies by mid-century all conformed to a general pattern of royal government, the province of Georgia falling into this category in 1752, with the lapse of the twenty-one year period of the charter under which it had been founded. Massachusetts alone enjoyed certain exceptional privileges and guaranteed rights under its charter of 1691. The council was not nominated but indirectly elected, the members being chosen by the general assembly; and the Crown's right to disallow legislation was limited to a period of three years after the Privy Council had received it.

Otherwise, royal government, as found in the majority of the provinces, was based upon the commissions issued to the governors at the time of their appointment in the form of letters patent under the great seal and upon the royal instructions which accompanied them.

The governor's commission 'contained the grant to him of all powers necessary for establishing and maintaining a provincial government. Without this royal grant there could be no legal political authority in the colony.'* Whereas the rights granted in a charter were perpetual, unless terminated by voluntary surrender or by established judicial processes following the issue of writs of *quo warranto* or *scire facias*, the powers granted to a governor were recoverable at the King's pleasure, and a new commission was necessary whenever a new governor was appointed.

The royal instructions to the governor were in some respects of even greater constitutional importance, for the first part of them, the so-called general instructions, might not unfairly be likened to a written constitution for the colony. Their contents included a list of the governor's council, followed by statements of its duties and powers and the regulations binding its activities. Then came articles treating of the elected assembly, in which its privileges were outlined and the forms and limitations of its legislative powers defined. Also dealt with were such matters as the administration of justice, inferior provincial officials, religion and morals, militia and local defence, maritime affairs, the land system, trade and com-

* L. W. Labaree, *Royal Government in America* (New Haven, 1930), p. 8.

merce, and the devolution of the government on the death, absence, or incapacity of the governor. Adjustments of a minor kind could be and were made when a new governor was appointed, but there was never any suggestion that privileges of representative government once conceded by the Crown and rendered prescriptive by long practice might be reduced. Nevertheless the general acceptance of these instruments concealed a potential clash of views between, on the one hand, colonists who thought of their assemblies as true parliaments which they enjoyed in virtue of their rights as Englishmen, and, on the other, the home government, which saw them as subordinate agencies derived from the authority of the Crown. The dynamics of colonial polity conflicted with the situation created by law.

Each royal governor held a key position in his colony as head of the local administration and as the link connecting the colony with the King's government in Britain. He had various, but not exclusive, responsibilities for appointing the other officials within his colony – though this prerogative was invaded both by the ministers at home and by the provincial assemblies. He had a general authority and responsibility for supervising the activities of the executive government within his province. This included the enforcement both of the law contained in provincial legislation and of British statutes extending to the colonies. In theory, but rarely in practice, he had full control of salaries and expenditure for government purposes. He also had full military and naval powers. His commission gave him the military authority virtually of a commander-in-chief; and he received a separate commission as vice-admiral. In discharge of all these various responsibilities he was bound by directions contained in his commission, in his general instructions, and in such particular instructions as might be issued to him on first appointment and thereafter from time to time. These last might be framed in accordance with the information concerning the affairs of his province which it was one of his duties to provide.

In many matters of administration the governor was required to act with the advice of his council. This body usually numbered about twelve. It was recruited from among prominent inhabitants of the colony, selected in the first instance by the governor himself, who was also required to keep the

home government provided with a short-list of reserves for
the immediate filling of vacancies due to death or other
cause. In the royal governments the council acted also as an
upper chamber of legislature; and the governor, as the
King's representative, gave or withheld assent to bills passed
by the assembly and council. As chief agent of the Crown
in his colony the governor was in constant correspondence
with the home government, chiefly with the secretary of
state or, after 1752, with the commissioners of the Board of
Trade.

On the whole the colonial governors during the eighteenth
century were men of comparatively high quality. They represented a fair cross-section of the public men of their age and
compared favourably in abilities and character with the
leading office-holders at home. Of those in office about 1750,
one at least, William Shirley of Massachusetts, might be
described as outstanding. Many of those appointed as governors had had considerable previous experience of the
colonies, usually in a military or a legal capacity, and showed
energy and enterprise in forwarding the interests of their
province; a few were colonial-born. A number of them won
great respect and affection in their colonies; and this was true
even of some of those who had the roughest political passage
in their relations with their assemblies.

In every colony the assembly was the institution expressing
local political energies and local separatism. It was thus inevitably in conflict with the local representative of the imperial
executive. By the mid-eighteenth century some of the principles and practices of imperial control had long vanished
before the insistent pressure of the assemblies; over others the
governors backed by the royal executive at home were fighting
a losing rearguard action. While the assemblies had secured
many of the privileges appertaining to the House of Commons,
in the royal colonies, generally speaking, the governors had
preserved the prerogative rights of adjournment, prorogation
and dissolution to a greater extent than was now the case in
Britain. In Massachusetts annual election of the assembly was
secured by the charter, and South Carolina and New Hampshire had local triennial acts. Elsewhere the assembly, once
summoned, might endure until the next demise of the Crown.
This right to retain a favourable body of representatives was

jealously guarded: between 1731 and 1752 the home government disallowed bills for limiting the duration of the assembly, submitted by the legislatures of New Jersey, North Carolina and New York.

Governors were under instruction that the laws which the legislatures of their provinces might make should be not repugnant but agreeable to the laws and statutes of Great Britain; and a parliamentary enactment of 1696 provided that any colonial act repugnant to British law or to any future statute extending to the colonies should be void. They had specific instructions about the use of their right of assent in many circumstances, acting as a first check upon the wishes of the assembly, while the government hovered as long-stop in the background at need. In those cases where the governor had no reason to withhold his assent to legislation, he was required to transmit all acts home for royal approval within three months of their passage, and the ministers, acting through the Privy Council, might thereupon exercise the Crown's right of disallowance, a veto which rendered an act void from the moment notice of it reached the colony. Except for the provisions in the charters of Pennsylvania and Massachusetts there was no time limit within which the decision to disallow must be taken. For convenience a practice had grown up during the eighteenth century of requiring the governor to reserve various classes of bills for the pleasure of the Crown. Under this process the governor neither vetoed nor approved a bill submitted to him by the two houses of the legislature but transmitted it for the process to be completed at home. Some bills he was instructed not to approve unless the Crown had given prior consent to their introduction into the legislature. Others were required to contain clauses suspending their operation until the royal approval had been received: these embraced among others the broad category of bills amending or repealing an existing approved law of the colony. Certain bills he was absolutely forbidden to approve.

But these shields and bucklers of imperial authority were vulnerable. For by the beginning of the eighteenth century the assemblies had firmly established two privileges of the first importance: the right to assent to laws and taxes, and the right to initiate legislation. The governors could not therefore evade the necessity for frequent and regular sessions; and the

assemblies could make their demands known and refuse to vote
funds for the support of government unless these were met.
Only in Maryland and in Virginia were there limited funds
available from permanent appropriations and quit-rents
which assured the salary of the governor and other senior
officials, but these were not sufficient to permit much executive
independence. Lacking guaranteed funds the governors were
unable to carry out their functions in any way which clashed
seriously with the popular wishes expressed in their assemblies
and were sometimes entirely deprived of executive powers.
Civil establishments defrayed from parliamentary grants
were not seriously considered. It was a basic principle of the
eighteenth-century Empire, that each province should provide
funds for its own government (only where this was imprac-
ticable, as in Nova Scotia and in Georgia did the home
authorities defray the cost of administration). But it was also
thought necessary that these funds should be under the control
of the royal representative. During the early years of the
century this policy appeared in the form of instructions to
governors that they should secure permanent provision for
civil government from their assemblies (just as Parliament
made permanent provision for the civil list in Great Britain).
But the assemblies were adamant. The analogy with British
conditions was false, for whereas the ministerial agents of the
King were by now firmly answerable to Parliament for the
way in which they conducted the administration, the colonial
governor owed his responsibility to London and was irrespon-
sible in his relations with his assembly save in so far as a
financial curb was imposed to make him amenable. In Massachusetts, New Hampshire, New York, New Jersey, and South
Carolina, the governor was dependent upon a salary voted
only for a year at a time.

Not only did the assemblies exploit this situation to coerce
the governors into policies which they desired, including the
giving of assent to bills even if this was forbidden by the
governor's instructions; but in some cases at least, they had
gone further by wholesale usurpation of executive functions.
This process had perhaps been pushed furthest in New York
and in Pennsylvania. In both provinces the assemblies had
insisted upon control of appropriations. They had also wrested
from the governor the power of appointing to various provin-

cial offices, particularly the offices in charge of provincial funds and credit, by such devices as the appropriation of salaries to officials by name and not by office. Almost everywhere similar practices developed. More generally, assemblies usurped governors' powers over Indian affairs by appointing their own agents for such business; controlled their discharge of military functions by dictating in appropriation acts where and when the provincial militia might be employed, and by appointing committees to supervise operations. The Privy Council complained in 1745, that the assembly of New York had assumed control of practically the entire executive branch of government. Of South Carolina Governor Glen remarked in 1748 that 'the people have the whole of the administration in their hands'. And the Board of Trade observed of Massachusetts in 1757: 'Almost every act of executive and legislative power, whether it be political, judicial, or military, is ordered and directed by votes of the General Court, in most cases originating with the House of Representatives.'*

Inevitably perhaps, British policies and attitudes with regard to the position of the colonial assemblies were inconsistent. On the one hand there was a consciousness of common interest seen from a central position of power, which it seemed only a central executive and legislature with full directing powers could secure. Then the aggressive behaviour and parochial outlook of the assemblies were resented and stress laid on their character as subordinate corporations deriving power from royal authority. On the other hand representative government was seen as a right that should be enjoyed. In fact the provinces were endowed with legislatures constructed on a parliamentary pattern, governor, council and house of assembly corresponding roughly with King, Lords, and Commons. At the same time as the home government continued to assert the doctrine that the assembly was a mere creature of grace and favour, it was insisting on its use in a way that suggested it was something more. This attitude is well illustrated by the ministers' reaction to the sudden realization, half-way through the Seven Years War, that although Nova Scotia had at last acquired a small number of British settlers, legislation was still being effected by the governor and a

*Cited Curtis P. Nettels, *The roots of American civilization* (2nd edn. N.Y., 1963), p. 564.

council alone. They insisted upon an assembly being constituted (1758), despite the governor's protests that there were
only enough Englishmen in the province to elect two representatives! Sir William Blackstone, a leading constitutional
authority of the day, lecturing in the 1750s on the government
of Great Britain and her colonies, wrote of 'their general
assemblies, which are their houses of commons'. When, even
to Englishmen at home, the similarity was thus apparent, it
is the more understandable that the colonists came to insist,
as they approached political maturity, that their legislatures
were not mere municipal councils but local parliaments, fully
competent to act in each colony as Parliament acted at home.

CHAPTER TWO

The Tests and Strains of War, 1754-1763

IN April 1754 a French expedition from Canada occupied the site of future Pittsburgh, forcing a Virginian garrison to surrender the half-completed fort they had begun to erect; and the great Anglo-French Nine Years' War for empire had begun. In February 1763 Parliament finally approved a peace treaty under which the French gave up all claims to territory on the American mainland. The position of the British Empire in America was transformed; but during these pregnant nine years there was a crystallization of tensions which were before long to lead to its violent collapse.

The most significant result of the war was the release of the mainland colonies from foreign European pressure and the threat of encirclement. The colonists' sense of dependence on British power was thus blunted and a brake on incipient separatist tendencies had been removed. On both sides of the Atlantic the great victories of the war bred a spirit of pride and self-confidence. At the same time as these feelings quickened the sense of self-sufficiency and independence among the colonists, they stimulated in official circles in London a trend towards closer organization and integration of the empire. Even during the course of the war, American particularism came face to face with imperial control, a series of incidents kindled a sense of dissatisfaction with the imperial relationship, the lines of cleavage which were to split the empire were virtually drawn, and problems of imperial organization were posed which led directly to the crisis of the Revolution.

The problem of the wilderness, otherwise the problem of Indian relations, was, in a way, a catalyst of Anglo-American conflict, for the uncoordinated and sometimes unscrupulous activities of the colonists beyond the areas of settlement led Whitehall to think in terms of unified imperial control, of an imposed frontier policy, and of imperial establishments to enforce it for which someone would have to pay. While this issue was in part shaped by Anglo-French rivalry on and to the south of the Great Lakes and the St. Lawrence, more long-term factors were also involved. Indian relations involved two things – commerce and land. Mishandled they could mean frontier warfare and devastation. It was patent, as reports of deteriorating relations with the Indians flowed into Whitehall in the early 'fifties, that a well-conceived, coordinated handling of these relationships was impossible, so long as each colony insisted upon its own local control of Indian affairs, and so long as factions within some of the colonies were divided over the correct policy to follow. Commercial interests in New York, Pennsylvania, Maryland, and Virginia were all, in varying degrees, in competition for the Indian trade in the region of the Great Lakes and the Ohio valley. Influential New Yorkers were divided between two groups. One favoured the renewal of a tacit 'neutrality' in any war in which French Canada might be involved. The other, more aggressive faction stood for an active patronage of the Indian Six Nations south of the upper St. Lawrence and the expulsion of the French from the areas to which they laid claim round the eastern Great Lakes. Expansionist groups in Pennsylvania were obstructed by the pacifist attitude of the dominant Quaker party, which had no stomach for the military consequences of a forward policy. The ruling elements of Virginian society were almost wholly committed to a policy of western expansion but were split among numerous competing groups of land speculators. Men from Virginia, Maryland, Pennsylvania and Connecticut all sought concessions in the area of the headstreams of the Ohio, rivalries bedevilled by uncertainty about the Pennsylvania boundary. Ordered diplomacy between the Indians on the one hand and the British on the other was thus impossible. The French thrust to the upper Ohio in 1753 and 1754 made this confused situation highly dangerous.

In accordance with instructions issued from London in September 1753, a conference of representatives of the colonies most threatened by the French initiative was convened at Albany, for the purpose of concluding a general treaty with the Six Nations for the restoration of amity. The proceedings merely emphasized the need for central imperial direction. New Jersey, having no exposed frontier, declined to take part; so did the Virginians, who expected to reap benefit from a separate conference of their own then in session with the Indians of the Ohio valley. Those delegates who were present did clearly see the need for some form of united executive authority to conduct Indian relations and defence. But their proposals, in any case too visionary for the home government to swallow, received short shrift from the colonial legislatures, most of which strongly condemned the proposed encroachments upon their powers of independent self-government. The Indians were mollified by gifts but saw no attraction in an alliance with the colonists whose political divisions made a unified defence policy impossible. Colonial disarray and maladroitness became overt when the delegates of Connecticut secretly negotiated a purchase of territory in the Wyoming valley, generally understood to be Pennsylvanian territory, at the same time as the Pennsylvanians themselves purchased lands extending beyond the watershed of the Allegheny range. These were deals into which the Indians were led in haste and then repented at leisure: colonial land-hunger, the threat to the hunting grounds, was the greatest cause of Indian diffidence.

Indian adherence to the French during the subsequent war underlined the need for a well-regulated and conciliatory Indian policy. The pacifist Quakers of Pennsylvania were the first to heed the lesson. At the treaty of Easton of 1758, by which the Indians of the upper Ohio were detached from the French, the Pennsylvanians ceded back the lands west of the Allegheny mountains included in their purchase of four years earlier and gave pledges that they would make no further grants for settlement in the area. This agreement was a crucial step towards the defeat of the French at Fort Duquesne (the future Pittsburgh). The wisdom of such a policy was further emphasized by the outbreak of a Cherokee war provoked by the expansion of British settlements in the interior of South Carolina. It lasted for two years and diverted appreciable regular military forces from the main theatre of war to the northward. By the peace of Ashley Ferry, which terminated it, the South Carolina authorities accepted a clause fixing a westward limit of British occupation. In similar response to the needs of the situation British military headquarters in the north gave several assurances to the Indians, that there would be no encroachments on their hunting grounds, and forceful steps were taken to remove a number of frontiersmen from

Virginia and Maryland who had proceeded to occupy lands yielded up by the Pennsylvanians at Easton. Virginian land speculators abated none of their pretensions, however, and during 1760 and 1761 the home government was involved in a long-drawn correspondence with the governor, urging the inexpediency of allowing settlement on any lands to which a completely free title had not been obtained with the full and willing consent of all the Indian peoples concerned. About the same time the government quickly withdrew assent it had given to extensions of settlement in northern New York, which had provoked a vigorous protest from the Mohawk Indians. By 1761 an imperial policy for the wilderness was emerging, which was in sharp conflict with both the aspirations of landless frontiersmen and the vested interests of many business groups involved in land speculation in the colonies. In that year a general instruction was sent to colonial governors, that no settlements or grants of land should be permitted which might interfere with Indians living on the borders of the provinces. All future applications for land-grants must stand referred to the Board of Trade. Meanwhile officials on the spot had themselves laid the foundations of a control of intercourse with the Indians, designed to reduce the friction arising from dishonest trading. With the advice of the New York frontier expert, William Johnson, the commander-in-chief placed the traffic under regulation. Only traders licensed through Johnson would be admitted to the Indian districts; and trade could only be carried on at a garrisoned post, where the local commander had the responsibility of seeing that the regulations were observed and of protecting the natives from any injustice.

A second major problem which began to loom large in the 'fifties was that of colonial currency. The clash which developed was one not merely over monetary policy but over constitutional powers, and it was considerably exacerbated by the course of the war.

In most of the provinces – Massachusetts after 1749 was a conspicuous exception* – the supply of specie was inadequate

*The favourable position of Massachusetts was due partly to the receipt in 1749 of £175,000 in specie from Great Britain as a reimbursement for its efforts in the previous French war, and partly through the considerable supply of silver obtained through trade with Portugal, Spain, and the Spanish West Indies.

to furnish a metal currency, and various shifts had been adopted to provide some alternative medium of exchange. One which operated effectively if under proper control was the issue of provincial bills of credit, normally drawing interest (which in some colonies practically defrayed the cost of local administration) and redeemable after a fixed term of years. The colonial need for currency of this kind was understood in London and no exception was taken to properly drafted legislation. But the home government was alert to check mismanagement. If maladministered this practice involved obvious perils of inflation: by the 'fifties Rhode Island had already succumbed and laid the seeds of its downfall as a commercial centre. Except perhaps for New Jersey, where the management of credit instruments was particularly scrupulous, no colony had entirely avoided this danger, and most provincial paper currencies were undergoing a slow depreciation of value in terms of sterling. After 1754 war expenditure gave the inflationary process a sharp impetus.

Inevitably debtor interests, especially in the tobacco colonies, attempted to exploit this situation by discharging their debts in depreciated currency. This was opposed by creditor interests in the main ports and by the general body of British merchants trading with America. Their demands for the full sterling value of all debts had the backing of the home government, which was thus drawn into conflict with a number of the colonial assemblies in which the debtor interests were preponderant. In 1749 a particularly provocative step was taken by the Virginia assembly when it passed a bill, confirmed unawares by the British authorities, providing that debts within the province might be paid in Virginia currency at the rate of £125 Virginia for every £100 sterling. As this figure was significantly below the current rate of exchange, there is little doubt that the bill reflected a deliberate attempt by the planter aristocracy who dominated the legislature to scale down their debts. As the bill was confirmed in London it could not be overthrown; and not until 1755, when the need for British support was very apparent, did the Virginia legislature give way to British representations and pass an amending bill, which empowered judges dealing with debtor cases to settle the rate of exchange in each given case. There was even sharper practice by the North Carolina legislature, where similar bills of 1748

and 1754 made bills of credit legal tender at a fixed value in
sterling. Inflation was such that by 1759 creditors could obtain
barely half the sterling value of their debts.

Against such practices the British authorities tried to impose
certain safeguards in currency acts: the inclusion of a suspensory clause; prohibition of any enactment that colonial paper
should be legal tender in which payment of debts must be
accepted; and the fixing of a fairly short time-limit, usually
not more than five years, within which bills of credit must be
redeemed. So far as the New England colonies were concerned
these principles were made statutory in the New England paper
money act passed by parliament in 1751. Otherwise they were
embodied in instructions to the governors. But just as the
government began to grasp the need for a policy, circumstances made a firm stand on the currency issue impossible.
Once the war began, colonial appropriations for the defence
of their frontiers were urgently required. The financial lever
gave the colonies the whiphand. From 1754 onwards most of
the assemblies regularly flouted the instructions about the
suspensory clause and the time-limit for redemption, and on
some occasions insisted on making their bills legal tender.
Regulations to the contrary were denounced as derogation of
the full legislative powers which they maintained were their
right. The assemblies also obliged governors to violate their
instructions by giving assent to finance bills by which the
moneys voted were placed in the control of their own nomi-
nees. In fact the war intensified the struggle in the colonies
over royal instructions, and the evasion of them caused
mounting irritation at home: in 1759, in a conversation with
Benjamin Franklin, the Lord President of the Council was
moved to forceful language on the subject.

The suspect nature of the Virginia currency legislation helps
to explain the course of a further currency crisis arising out of
the so-called Virginia 'two-penny act'. In this province (and
also in Maryland) tobacco notes issued to cover deposits of
tobacco in public warehouses were widely used as currency.
This had led to a regular practice of stipulating in private
contracts and public acts for payment in pounds of tobacco
rather than in money. But a bad crop could cause a violent
upward leap in the price of tobacco. By 1753 the Virginia
legislature adopted the expedient of a temporary enactment

permitting the discharge of tobacco obligations at a money equivalent near to the price current in good years. In 1758, the third recent occasion of crop failure, the legislature fixed the equivalent at twopence a pound. A clause in the bill required vendors of tobacco under contracts by which they had already received payments in advance at a higher rate either to fulfil the contract by delivering the tobacco or to pay back an amount equal to that received. Contrary to his instructions the governor gave his assent to the bill, although it did not include a suspensory clause.

The bill offended two interests. It favoured debtors who had taken payment under contract for tobacco yet to be delivered at a price below what became current at the height of the shortage. These could now legally repudiate their contracts by returning cash and might then sell their crop at the higher price. This increased cost thus fell upon the British purchasers, who felt cheated and presented petitions against the act. Their pleas were reinforced by others from the Anglican clergy of the province, who complained that since they had been paid in tobacco when its price was low they were entitled to benefit when the price rose. On both these scores the British authorities considered the act to be unjust; it had in any case been passed contrary to instruction; and it was therefore disallowed. The governor was sternly warned to abide by his instructions; and upon learning this the Virginia assembly addressed a strong plea to the King for freedom to legislate without restriction in case of immediate necessity.

The twopenny act has been both praised and condemned by American historians.* On the one hand, some protection to tobacco debtors may have been necessary; though the picture sometimes presented of a planter class, sunk in debt to British merchants, driven to debt-reducing legislation in order to avert ruin, goes ill with the descriptions which exist of the extravagant and luxurious conditions in which many of them lived and which suggest that retrenchment would have been

---

*For a favourable view of Virginia currency legislation, see, for example, C. P. Nettels, *Roots of American Civilization* (2nd edn., N.Y., 1963), pp. 419–23, 597–8; B. Knollenberg, *Origin of the American Revolution, 1759–1766* (N.Y., 1961), pp. 57, 66. Critical of it is L. H. Gipson, *The Coming of the Revolution, 1763–1775* (1954), pp. 47–9, and *The British Empire before the American Revolution*, X, pp. 168–79.

a practicable and more respectable way of making ends meet. On the other, the merchants were suddenly faced with an artificial tampering with the price mechanism to their disadvantage; and there seems to have been a genuine basis for grievance on the part of the clergy, who were accustomed to trade their tobacco dues to British merchants as payment for debts and found themselves with nothing in hand but depreciated colonial currency. There was no recourse to such action in neighbouring Maryland.

But whatever the rights or wrongs of the act in economic and fiscal terms, one salient fact stands out. In demanding freedom to pursue an independent monetary policy the Virginian legislature was asserting claims incompatible with membership of a single polity. As the affair was protracted by lawsuits brought by some of the clergy in an attempt to recover their lost dues, these claims were reiterated with increasing stridency. In one notable law-case in 1763 the young Virginian lawyer, Patrick Henry, attacked the royal disallowance as an exercise of tyrannical power contrary to the contractual relation between king and people. He denounced the 'bondage' of people who were denied the privilege of enacting their own laws and maintained that the Virginia legislature was the only body with authority to make law for the province. In one of the pamphlets provoked by the controversy the senior burgess of the house of representatives declared in similar vein: 'Submission, even to the supreme magistrate, is not the whole duty of a citizen . . . Something is likewise due to the rights of our country and to the liberties of mankind. To say that a royal instruction to a governor, for his own particular conduct, is to have the force and validity of a law, and must be obeyed, without reserve, is, at once, to strip us of the rights and privileges of British subjects, and to put us under the despotic power of a French or Turkish government, for what is the real difference between a French edict and an English instruction if they are both equally absolute.'* The logical projection of the claim to 'the rights and privileges of British subjects' was complete independence of any restraint by a power external to the province.

Another focus of conflict was provided by the courts of law. The colonial law courts of the 'fifties might be regarded

*Cited in Knollenberg, p. 66.

as one of the last lines of defence for British authority. The ways in which judges might direct attention to evidence or decide doubtful points of law could determine whether imperial policies would be enforced or ignored. In the charter colonies the game was already lost: judges who owed their appointments directly or indirectly to popular choice systematically evaded decisions involving enforcement of imperial regulations contrary to public opinion. Elsewhere the home government was anxious that as much jurisdiction as possible should be centred in superior courts which were less likely to be swayed by local sentiment, and it consistently disallowed colonial acts for extending the jurisdiction of county courts. In the royal governments it tried to secure for the judges as great a degree as possible of independence from local pressures. Between 1759 and 1761 this policy led to a controversy over the tenure of judges and the provision of their salaries. Hitherto the British practice of appointing judges 'during good behaviour' – in effect for life – had not been extended to the colonies. For the most part the judges in the royal colonies held appointment at pleasure. The British case for maintaining this element of control was that, in many instances, judges were dependent upon salaries voted annually by the colonial assembly and were thus exposed to financial pressure if they clashed with popular opinion. Between 1759 and 1761, in order to obviate this objection, the assemblies of New York, Pennsylvania, and North Carolina passed bills making provision for permanent salaries provided the judges were appointed during good behaviour. But by this time other considerations were swaying government policy, and these proposals were rejected, as likely to lessen the 'dependence which the colonies ought to have upon the government of the Mother Country.'*

Meanwhile the French war raised specifically in a more urgent form than hitherto the twin problems of imperial defence and finance. The struggle against the French and their Indian allies, in a theatre of war of enormous distances and difficult terrain, exacted an unprecedented military effort in America and a correspondingly enormous expense. Traditionally colonial contribution was by 'requisition'. The crown

*Report of the Board of Trade, 11 Nov. 1761, *Acts of the Privy Council, Colonial Series*, IV, 498–500, cited Knollenberg, p. 73.

demanded assistance from each colony in rough proportion
to its resources. But supply depended upon the goodwill of
the colonial legislatures, and if a provincial assembly refused
to comply there was no way of compelling it to act. During the
war the government adopted with some effect a policy of
incentives: reimbursements were granted by Parliament to
each colony in proportion to the supply raised there during
the previous year, and over the period of the whole war
perhaps two-fifths of the total military outlay of the colonies
was made good in this way. Furthermore the government
undertook to supply arms, ammunition, artillery, tents, and
provisions, provided the colonies recruited adequate numbers
of men and clothed and paid them – an arrangement which
surmounted the considerable difficulty of raising troops in
Britain and eliminated the need for shipping to carry such
troops to America.

For most of the war certain colonies responded exceptionally
well under this system: Massachusetts, Connecticut and New
York contributed generously, but the fact that their appropriations provided seven-tenths of all the funds raised in
America revealed the general inadequacy of the method of
requisition. In the seaboard colonies with no stake in the
interior – Rhode Island, New Jersey, and Delaware – local
particularism far outweighed any sense of a common imperial
cause. Quaker pacifism was a main factor in the reluctance to
vote supplies in Pennsylvania. New Hampshire and North
Carolina were conspicuous for pleading poverty as an excuse
for non-compliance with requisitions. Neither Virginia nor
Maryland contributed so much relative to their populations
and other resources as the three northern colonies first mentioned above. The war effort was hampered by the mutual
jealousy with which various assemblies compared their contributions with their neighbours', and some insisted upon
making appropriations contingent upon the performances of
other provinces.

Provincial particularism also blocked the proper strategic
deployment of colonial troops. It was an understood principle
(also observed in Britain) that militia service was for home
defence only, and that the militia might only be employed
outside their own borders with the consent of the provincial
authority. The consequences of rigid adherence to it are well

revealed by the story of Fort Cumberland, a post of crucial importance for operations in the direction of the upper Ohio. The Virginians consistently refused to provide a garrison on the ground that the fort lay in territory claimed by Maryland, but the Marylanders equally disclaimed ownership or any obligation to provide troops; and so regulars had to be kept back from offensive operations to make the place secure.

On occasion New England recruits were loth to come forward, unless they knew they would be under a commander they trusted and would not be required to serve to the southward. Sometimes assemblies insisted that their troops should serve under one particular commander, and no other, and should be used only for certain specified operations. When, for one reason or another, appropriations proved inadequate and funds for pay ran short, colonial troops were likely to go off home before the campaign was over, and save in one or two provinces there was no effective law for the enforcement of military discipline or the rounding up of deserters. To recruit good fighting men, or even to recruit men at all, was difficult except in some of the northern colonies. The ordinary colonist was under no economic pressure to enrol in the militia and effective measures of conscription were unacceptable. Recruitment therefore depended upon liberal bounties and pay, and few of the assemblies were prepared to offer them. Save in the north volunteers were generally of poor quality, drawn from the shiftless and least enterprising sections of the population. In their correspondence British officers habitually expressed contempt for them. Even the men of better calibre were often too individualistic ever to be reconciled to military discipline or to the more humdrum tasks of military life. It proved almost impossible to confine them in garrisons. Washington was obliged to confess his inability in 1756 to prevent the Virginia militia sent to guard the frontier from deserting almost *en masse*. In a well-known passage he sketched a deplorable picture of the demoralization and irresponsibility of the frontier settlers: 'When Hampshire was invaded and called upon Frederick [county] for assistance, the people of the latter refused their aid, answering, "let them defend themselves as we shall do if they come to us". Now the enemy have forced through that country and begin to infest this, those a little removed from danger are equally infatuated; and will be, I fear, until all in turn fall a sacrifice to an insulting and merciless enemy.'*

Another circumstance which increased the ministers' dissatisfaction with the existing system of defence was the determination of a number of the colonial assemblies to exploit the emergency, in order to win further powers for themselves in both legislative and executive matters, in defiance of the authority of Parliament, the Crown, the governors as the Crown's representatives, and, in the proprietary colonies, of the proprietors also. The ensuing controversies involved the delay and sometimes the complete withholding of military appropriations. Assemblies refused to comply with the rule for redemption of bills of credit within five years or for the inclusion of a suspending clause in the bills authorizing issue and insisted on bills becoming legal tender. In some cases at least it seems clear that these steps were not due to deliberate desire for an inflationary policy so much as to resentment at the denial of complete legislative freedom represented by the governor's instructions. In Maryland and Pennsylvania, where imperial interests were almost entirely over-shadowed by the internal political conflicts, the attack was aimed at the special privileges claimed by the proprietors. The Pennsylvania assembly insisted on including in tax bills the personal estates of the Penns; and when, in 1760, their fiscal legislation was disallowed on this and other grounds, they declined to vote any further funds for the war except on the same terms. In Maryland the assembly (on good grounds) called in question the proprietor's claim to revenues from fines and licenses, insisted that these belonged to the province, and obliged him to give way before they would vote any sums for defence. They also carried in 1757 an act, contrary to his instructions to the governor, levying a tax upon his estates. A little later they produced a complete deadlock by presenting the governor with an elaborate bill, incompatible with his instructions, for taxing real and personal property, offices, professions, proprietary quit-rents and ecclesiastical preferments, and for putting control of the troops so provided in the hands of special commissioners chosen by themselves. The

---

*For the inadequate provision for colonial defence in 1755, 1756 and 1757, see L. H. Gipson, *The British Empire before the American Revolution*, vol. VI, pp. 11–16, 44–54, 64–72; VII, pp. 34–61, 140–49.

governor had no choice but to withhold assent, and from that time Maryland contributed scarcely any funds for the prosecution of the war.

The contrast between the performances of the charter colonies and of the proprietary colonies is instructive, though the lesson seems to have been missed at the time. Connecticut, virtually a commonwealth unto itself, and Massachusetts, where the charter ensured exceptional popular control of administration, showed a strong sense of the general imperial interest and contributed to it better than the other colonies. Provinces where the assemblies felt they had grievances, in the form of denial of rights of self-government arising out of instructions to the governors and the surveillance over their legislation of the Crown, tended to put redress of these complaints before the general imperial interest; and the situation was worst where the grievances were directed not only against the Crown but against the proprietors. Where the evolution of the Empire had proceeded furthest towards a commonwealth pattern, there responsibilities had been most fully accepted – with the one exception, as will be seen below – of the little charter colony of Rhode Island.

Finally the war provoked new contentions over trade.

During the eighteenth century the northern colonies had built up a highly lucrative traffic with the French settlements in the West Indies and in the St. Lawrence valley, exchanging surpluses of provisions and lumber for island produce, particularly for molasses, the indispensable raw material for rum. Under British law this commerce did not become illegal until the formal declaration of war in 1756, two years after hostilities had broken out on the Ohio. And yet provisions from the British colonies were of vital concern to the French on their northern borders: it was at one time reported, that French troops on the Ohio were being sustained by stores bought at Louisberg in French Cape Breton Island and shipped up the St. Lawrence. Correspondence of colonial officials included the report, that on one occasion in 1755 no less than forty ships, chiefly from New York, Rhode Island, and Massachusetts, had been seen together in Louisberg harbour. In the course of the year, however, most of the colonial executives took steps to suppress this traffic by embargoes on the export of provisions or by other means.

After 1756 direct trade with the French West Indies was illegal, but despite naval interceptions a good deal was carried on illicitly and various means of evasion were practised. The Rhode Islanders in particular openly flouted the law. In Pennsylvania the trade was continued by a flagrant abuse of cartel ships, sailing under flag of truce ostensibly for the exchange of prisoners, in which the governor himself openly connived. The Rhode Islanders also adopted this device. More serious, however, was the general switching of the trade through neutral ports in the West Indies, At first the Dutch entrepôt of St. Eustatius was used; but when the navy systematically seized, as contraband, cargoes of foodstuffs *en route* from there to French bases in Dutch ships, a new centre of exchange was developed at Monte Cristi on Hispaniola, on the Spanish side of the frontier with French Haiti. Here goods were regularly trans-shipped from British to French vessels. Although this traffic was in flagrant defiance of the law against trade with the enemy, officials in the colonial ports long hesitated to refuse clearance papers, since the merchants were technically within the law in sending their ships to a neutral port. From 1759, however, the navy interfered vigorously, the local vice-admiralty courts accepting the view that British ships thus breaking the spirit of the law should be condemned to its penalties; but it was never able to suppress it entirely. By this trade colonial merchants gave substantial aid and comfort to the enemy. The French West Indian bases were sustained with supplies which could not have been obtained from any other source. The British capture of Louisberg was retarded for at least a year because by this means the French fleet was able to re-provision. Such were the consequences of the merchants' determination to maintain to the full their profitable importation of French molasses and sugar which the desperate need of provisions in the French islands made even more lucrative. The scale on which they supplied French wants was such that the British forces in America at times found difficulty in obtaining provisions, and the (illegally) imported French sugar – subsequently passed off as British in consignments to London and Bristol – seriously affected the exports of sugar from Jamaica and other British islands to the mainland colonies.

In 1760, in default of better means, colonial executives

began to strike at this trade by enforcement of the Molasses Act of 1733.* The duties imposed by that Act were intended to be prohibitive. Even if colonial shippers importing from Monte Cristi could evade prosecution for trading with the enemy, at least the molasses and sugars of French origin might be made so unattractive by exaction of the duties as to drive them to cheaper legitimate sources, which would benefit the British islands. At New York and at Boston enforcement was fairly successful; but much resentment was caused, owing to the continued evasion in Rhode Island, where the popularly elected law-enforcement officers and magistrates were on the side of the smugglers and the customs house officials were therefore powerless. The consequent bitterness and jealousy of the Boston merchants seems to have been the main factor behind a campaign of defiance about the beginning of 1761. Customs officials in Massachusetts were harassed, or threatened with harassment, by common-law actions for damages arising out of their attempts to enforce the Act; and after the death of George II steps were taken to block the re-issue of writs of assistance.

Writs of assistance empowered customs officers accompanied by a local peace officer to enter warehouses, stores, or homes during daylight hours, by force if necessary, to search on mere suspicion for smuggled goods. Unlike the ordinary process of a search warrant, no information had to be sworn, and the name of the informant could be concealed – an important consideration in view of the danger of reprisals. In 1755 such writs had been issued by the superior court of Massachusetts, at the instance of the governor, as a means of checking the trade with the French at Cape Breton Island, and others were granted in connection with the enforcement of the Molasses Act. Their authority ended with the death of George II, and when application was made to the superior court, the Boston merchants made legal representations against their renewal. There were in fact legal grounds for doubting the authority of the court to issue them, though for the moment the right to do so was affirmed and exercised. But what caught the public imagination in Boston was not the grave discussion of technicalities by the senior lawyers but an outpouring of rhetoric by the young barrister, James Otis, who declared that writs

*On the Molasses Act, see pages 10–11 above.

of assistance were 'against the fundamental principles of law' and that acts of parliament authorizing them, being contrary to the constitution and natural equity, were void. The popularity of this doctrinal challenge to the legal supremacy of parliament, in a matter touching the material interests of many of the merchants, was such that, although writs of assistance were re-issued, it proved impossible in defiance of public opinion ever again to use them.

These troubles over the trade, direct or indirect, with the enemy brought home a number of considerations to the imperial government. The weak state of the customs service in the colonies stood plainly revealed. In part this was due to corruption. Numbers of junior officers had ignored their duty and connived actively in illegal trade. But in part also it was due to inability to get support from the civil power, owing to the pressure of public opinion in favour of smuggling, and because officials from the lowest even to the rank of judge or governor might be implicated. War experience also underlined the value of the navy as a preventive service. A natural ministerial desire to put things right was intensified by officialdom's sense of outrage at the continuance of a traffic which had undoubtedly helped the enemy and perhaps prolonged the war. It was evident that an important section of the commercial interests in the northern colonies was more intent on profits than on the national interest. Patriotism dictated a breaking-off of the French trade. Even though this entailed losses these might be compensated by new opportunities created by the war, owing to the funds brought into the colonies from Britain with the army and the great demand for timber and provisions which it created. Moreover, in 1759 the rich French island of Guadeloupe was brought by capture into the ambit of legitimate trade. It would perhaps be incorrect to read into the existence of the large-scale illicit traffic any marked degree of separatist feeling: smuggling was common enough in Britain also. But it had significance on at least two grounds. It was one of a number of factors leading to a post-war imperial policy of greater centralization; and at the same time the popular response to Otis's speech reflected the growing intensity of colonial resentment at central control of any kind.

CHAPTER THREE

A Policy for America, 1763-1765

WITH the ratification of the peace treaty in February 1763 the affairs of America emerged as one of the outstanding post-war problems facing the British government. The retirement of the Earl of Bute in April left this responsibility in the hands of the administration headed by his protégé, George Grenville.

Grenville was a commanding figure in politics, an indefatigable worker, respected in parliament for his political and personal integrity and for his thorough knowledge of questions of trade and public finance. But he lacked the warm humanity and imaginative grasp essential to the handling of imperial concerns in 1763. George III, who never liked him and finally declared that he would rather see the Devil in his closet, made one of his more discerning assessments of character when he remarked: 'that gentleman's opinions are seldom formed from any other motives than such as may be expected to originate in the mind of a clerk in a counting house.' However, in fairness to Grenville it must be said that this criticism came from one no more perceptive than he was of the intricacies of the colonial problem; and it must be remembered that Grenville faced a parliament anxious to see cuts in the heavy war-time rates of taxation.

During the two years of Grenville's ministry – from April 1763 till July 1765 – his leadership gave strong and purposeful direction to the central government. A new degree of compression was achieved in the cabinet, now narrowed down to nine ministers instead of twelve or more. An inner ring provided momentum and policy-direction. This consisted at first of Grenville and the two secretaries of state, Lord Egremont and Lord Halifax. After Egremont's death in August 1763 it came to include both his successor, the Earl of Sandwich, and the new Lord President, the Duke of Bedford.

The inner group reflected considerable continuity and in some cases depth of ministerial experience. All these leading ministers had held cabinet office during the last two or three years of the French war. Egremont had had continuous charge of colonial affairs since succeeding Pitt as southern secretary in October 1761. The general influence of Halifax in discussions of colonial affairs was probably even more important. An able and diligent professional politician, Halifax has had a certain notoriety as the man successfully prosecuted for unlawful arrest by John Wilkes. It is less frequently recalled that he gave his name to the chief port of Nova Scotia. His appointment as secretary of state in 1762 had been preceded by over twelve years' service as First Commissioner of the Board of Trade. During that time he had raised the Board well above its old standing as a mere office of report to a status not far short of a full executive department, had secured his own entrance into the cabinet while still at its head, and had won praise as 'father of the colonies' for his success in fostering American trade. He thus brought to the cabinet an intimate knowledge of and intense interest in colonial affairs, for which he became officially responsible on his transfer to the southern department after Egremont's death. In particular he had personal knowledge of the many reports in which colonial officials had drawn attention to the quasi-independence asserted by the colonial legislatures and to the inadequacies of the requisition system as a means of financing colonial defence.

The other two chief figures in Grenville's cabinet after the death of Egremont, Sandwich and Bedford, both had long and varied ministerial experience, particularly in diplomacy and in naval affairs. Neither had had much to do with the colonies, but Bedford's enthusiasm for imperial expansion had been apparent during his headship of the Admiralty during the last years of the war of the Austrian succession. Both favoured in principle the strengthening of the central imperial authority.

There were two chief elements in the problem presented by America in 1763: first, the government and defence of the new territories and, second, the provision of funds for these services.

The ministers' approach to the first of these questions developed naturally from the practical measures already taken by officials on the spot and explained and defended in their dispatches. Their ideas were probably confirmed rather than modified by the outbreak of the Indian war known as the 'conspiracy of Pontiac' which ravaged the frontiers of the middle colonies for nearly a year from May of 1763.

The origins of this Indian rising were complex and the relative weight to be given to various contemporary explanations of it remains obscure. But there is no doubt that the chief general cause was the apprehension created among the Indians of the Ohio region by the expulsion of French power from the American continent. They could no longer, as hitherto, try to balance one of the European nations against the other and hope to win survival out of their rivalries. They resented and feared the consequences of the transfer from France to Great Britain by the treaty of Paris of sovereignty over vast extents of territory defined as parts of either French Canada or Louisiana, which they had never conceded to be in French possession. The establishment of various British military posts on the Great Lakes and in the Illinois country appeared plain evidence of a British intention to hold them in subjection, and the decision of the British commander-in-chief in America, Sir Jeffrey Amherst, to withhold customary presents of shot and gunpowder seemed intended to weaken their potential fighting power. For years they had had good reason to fear the pressure of British westward migration, and these fears were intensified by rumours of new projected settlements, especially when Amherst temporarily encouraged the establishment of one to support the strategically important garrison at Niagara. Unscrupulous treatment by British traders added to their grievances. French agents working from St. Louis on the Mississippi were suspected of stirring up the tribes. Whatever the causes, in May 1763 the Ohio frontier burst into flame, Indian bands seized the outlying posts on and south of the Great Lakes, and by June they were pressing hard on the frontiers of Virginia, Maryland, and Pennsylvania. In the massacres of the next few months perhaps some two thousand settlers lost their lives.

Before 1754 Indian wars had been treated as a purely colonial responsibility. But in view both of the scale of the Pontiac rising and of the fact that the British had recently been fighting Indians in French pay, it was natural that the imperial government and its military representative should assume some degree of responsibility for defence of the frontier.

However, Amherst had neither enough regulars available, nor were they near the threatened area: many of the troops sent to America to fight the French had been withdrawn after 1761 to other theatres of war. The outlying posts had been held merely by handfuls of men intended to police rather than to garrison the interior. Only Detroit, Niagara, and Fort Pitt were strongly held and able to defy Indian attack. A major effort in self-defence was required from the colonies; but once again an unhappy impression was created in Whitehall of the colonists' inability or unwillingness to combine and contribute effectively, and it was twelve months before peace was restored. According to the requisitions made in November 1763, at the height of the crisis, by Amherst's successor, General Gage, New York and New Jersey were to furnish two thousand militia for the next year's campaign and fifteen hundred men were to be drawn from Pennsylvania and Virginia. In the event New York provided only three hundred of the fourteen hundred men reckoned as its share and New Jersey less than half the six hundred demanded. Pennsylvania voted a thousand men, but owing to delays in recruiting and subsequent desertions the campaigning season was nearly over before they were ready to move. Still worse from the viewpoint of the imperial government, the Virginia assembly refused to vote any troops for an offensive campaign and insisted that its militia should be used solely to hold defensive positions on the frontier. Counting the regulars available the campaign of 1764 had to be carried on without half the number of troops considered necessary. The whole affair probably made no difference to the main lines of the government's policy, which were already taking shape when Grenville succeeded at the Treasury. But it may well have confirmed ministers in their opinions about the best way to deal with the financial issues involved in their policy for America.

Plans for the government of the conquered American territories were tossed to and fro between Egremont's office and the Board of Trade during the summer of 1763 and were brought to completion by Halifax in the autumn. The conquests fronting the Caribbean were erected into the two new provinces of East and West Florida. Areas south of the St. Lawrence estuary were absorbed into the existing colony of Nova Scotia. Those further up the river, centred on Quebec

and Montreal, were thrown into a separate new colony of
Quebec. There remained the wilderness west of the upper St.
Lawrence and the watershed of the Appalachians. In this area
most of the old colonies had competing claims and interests,
based in some cases upon their original charters. Groups of
speculators, particularly in Virginia, Pennsylvania, and New
York, were concerned with plans, often mutually exclusive, for
the opening up of the Ohio valley.

In dealing with this region the problem which most exercised the British ministers was Indian relations. Their main
object was to secure peace between the two races. In the spring
of 1763 it was patent from the reports coming in from America
that there was no prospect of this, unless the government
confirmed the check upon westward settlement already
imposed by the officials on the spot and the steps they had
taken to control contact between the Indians and British
traders. From the viewpoint of Whitehall the land problem
was the less acute, because there seemed ample space for
excess population in the Floridas, in Nova Scotia, and in
Quebec. A population build-up in the south would provide
hands for the production of sub-tropical produce and would
strengthen the defences of the Empire on its southern flank
where it fronted the Spanish islands and the Spanish Main.
An influx of settlers in the north would permit exploitation of
valuable timber resources and would provide a safeguard
against the French *habitants* who might still nurse a loyalty to
France. Westward expansion therefore could be checked to
such a slow pace as would assure the fullest agreement with
the Indians over each release of land for settlement. A few
officials and a few speculative thinkers questioned the desira-
bility of westward expansion on other grounds. Some expressed fears that the high cost of carriage into the interior
would cause remote settlements to set up manufactures in
competition with those at home. Others pointed out the
difficulty of governing colonies at such distances inland. A few
feared that if the Empire were allowed to expand into the
interior it would soon become too powerful to hold. There is
no indication, however, that these considerations entered into
the shaping of imperial policy in 1763.

The outline of the new policy for the interior was made
public in the Proclamation of October 1763 (by which also

the new governments in Quebec and the Floridas were established). The Appalachian watershed was fixed 'for the present'
as the western boundary of British settlement. For the time
being no purchases of lands beyond this line would be authorized. In view of the urgent need to reassure the Indians now
up in arms on the frontier, the original intention of laying down
a provisional line to be surveyed subsequently in detail so as
to provide for certain limited areas of new settlement was
abandoned and an inconvenient rigidity imposed on the
frontier. Further north a similar limit of settlement was
imposed at the western edge of the Ottawa basin. The western
claims of the old colonies were not extinguished, but it was
provided that for the time being the administration of the
wilderness should be vested in the commander-in-chief in
America and that commercial dealings with the Indians should
be placed under regulation. This last provision confirmed the
war-time improvisation, under which Sir William Johnson
and John Stuart acted as Indian superintendents in the north
and south respectively, and, with a small devoted band of
helpers, tried to enforce the licensing of all British traders
and make them trade only at certain recognized centres where
their activities would be under surveillance – the Indian
villages in the south, the military outposts in the north. In
the following year the Board of Trade elaborated regulations
for this embryo Indian department, but lack of funds checked
its development.

This policy involved brushing aside, at least for the present,
the expansionist aims of various sections of colonial society.
It meant also the maintenance of costly military detachments
in Indian country – and the expense of supporting such remote
garrison posts was to prove even greater than had been expected. This charge was, however, only a part of the burden
of defence posed by the American Empire after 1763. The
main military dispositions must cover the northern and
southern flanks from the possibility of attack by France or
Spain. Had the government adopted the very different policy
– which it seems never to have contemplated – of abandoning
the interior and the defence of the Indian frontier to the
settled colonies, defence costs would have been reduced. But
they would still have been substantial, and they would have
still raised the fatal questions: should not the colonists con-

tribute a share of this charge and, for lack of other effective means of ensuring its collection, must not this share be raised by imperial authority?

The ministers' approach to this problem is understandable. For years colonial officials had been bombarding Whitehall with reports to the effect that only by imperial taxation could a proper defence contribution be secured from the colonies. The requisition system was unsatisfactory. While it had worked well with Massachusetts, Connecticut, and New York during the recent war, back-sliding colonies could and did evade their obligations. The principle that the colonies should contribute to defence in time of war was firmly established. It was true that contributions had not hitherto been asked for in peacetime, but circumstances alter cases – it was necessary to be prepared, on the assumption that the Bourbon powers would try to reverse the decision of 1763 if they saw opportunity – and it was natural for Grenville and his colleagues to view imperial taxation as a more effective extension of the principle. Even before the peace treaty was ratified the Bute government had committed itself to this policy. Comparison of the fiscal situation in Britain and in the colonies made such a plan seem no more than equitable. When Grenville took over the Treasury, he was faced on the one hand with estimates for the defences of America and the West Indies amounting to over £300,000 annually, of which £200,000 was wanted for the mainland, and on the other with the fact that during the late war the national debt had doubled to what seemed the crippling figure of almost £140,000,000. The annual debt charge alone was between four and five millions. New sources of revenue had to be found – one consequence in Britain was the highly unpopular cider tax. By contrast, in the colonies domestic tax burdens were light, sometimes negligible, and most of the provinces could look forward to the complete retirement of their public war-debts within five or six years. It was not unreasonable for Grenville and his colleagues to regard the colonies as well able and morally obliged to share the burden of their own defence – a view to which some recent scholarship has given strong support.*

The first stage of Grenville's schemes was the exploitation

*L. H. Gipson, *The Coming of the Revolution, 1763-1775* (1954), chapters 9 and 10.

for revenue purposes of the existing Acts of Trade, which
imposed customs duties on goods entering America with the
object of controlling commerce. Prominent among these was
the Molasses Act of 1733, under which a significant revenue
had been collected since the beginning of war-time enforcement in 1760. Senior customs officials who had hitherto
treated their posts as sinecures suddenly found themselves
obliged to take up residence in America or else face dismissal.
Strict orders for the enforcement of the Acts were issued.
Revenue officers' powers were increased by an Act extending
to the colonies the right to seize ships 'hovering' offshore. The
scope of preventive activity was greatly increased by a provision that captains and officers of men-of-war in American
waters might be sworn in as customs officers with full powers
to seize and prosecute violaters of the laws of trade. During
the summer some forty vessels were deployed along the North
American coast, and their officers, stimulated by the statutory
reward of a share in the profits from sale of condemned cargoes,
pursued their new calling with such draconic zeal as to interfere grievously with legitimate coastal traffic. The sudden
rigid enforcement of a network of legal restrictions, hitherto
either wholly neglected or else treated with happy-go-lucky
attention to practical convenience, caused considerable em-
barrassment to the mercantile society of the Atlantic coast.

During the following year Grenville planned and, in part,
carried out a comprehensive overhaul of the laws of trade, in
which commercial and fiscal objects were closely interlinked.
This reform was enacted in the Plantation Act (popularly
known as the Sugar Act) of 1764. This statute reduced to 3d.
per gallon the duty on foreign molasses imported into America
previously fixed at the supposedly prohibitive level of 6d. by
the Molasses Act of 1733. Linked with this measure was the
imposition of a prohibitively high duty on the entry of foreign
refined sugar and an absolute prohibition on the entry of
foreign rum. These clauses were intended to balance the
divergent interests of the West India planters, the New England
rum distillers, and the British Treasury. The second conceded
an American monopoly to the planters. The third gave a
monopoly to the colonial distillers. The first made some concession to colonial complaint that the molasses duty was ruin-
ously high but also served two other purposes: to give British

West Indian molasses a favoured position in competition with that from the French islands; and to secure an ample revenue, since large quantities of foreign molasses were required by the American rum industry over and above what the British islands could supply. The Act also imposed duties on madeira wine imported direct from the Azores, which favoured both British wine shippers and colonial distillers; on coffee and pimiento exported from the newly acquired islands to other colonies; and on certain classes of oriental and French textiles imported via British ports, the use of which was still absolutely prohibited in Britain. Drawbacks payable on various foreign goods re-exported from Britain to the colonies were reduced.* British wine and textile exporters were expected to benefit from some of these provisions. Other commercial benefits was sought by placing coffee, pimiento, coconuts, whalefins, deerskins, iron, and timber on the 'enumerated list' of goods which, save for special exceptions, could not be exported from the colonies direct to a foreign market but only to Britain. At the same time, by other legislation, advantages of various kinds were held out to the colonists. Bounties were provided for the production of hemp and flax, and were continued, though at a lower rate than hitherto, for the indigo produced in South Carolina. Leave was given to export rice from this colony to any part of Latin America. The remission of nearly all the duties on the import of whalefins from the colonies into Britain offered a virtual monopoly to the New England whale fishers against both their Dutch and British competitors. A year later, in rectification of a serious error in the Plantation Act, the restriction on export of colonial timber was relaxed to permit the resumption of a profitable trade in barrel staves with Portugal and with Ireland, and at the same time a bounty on export to Britain was granted.

Of the fiscal provisions of the Sugar Act it was the molasses duty which aroused most complaint in the mainland colonies. Politicians in every generation have found the liquor trade the tetchiest of interests to meddle with, and George III's ministers were no exception. A great cry went up in America, that with the molasses duty fixed as high as 3d. the rum trade

*A drawback was a repayment, at the time of export, of duties which the revenue services had received, either as customs when goods were imported from abroad or as excise at the time of manufacture in Britain.

would be priced out of business and every other economic activity dependent upon it would likewise be ruined. Scholars are not yet in agreement over the degree of truth in these complaints. The more orthodox course has been to take them seriously. On the other hand a convincing case can be made against them. The wide spread between wholesale and retail prices of rum in the colonies at that time is indicative of ample profits capable of bearing substantial taxation. As for exports, it has been observed: 'What the retail price for this commodity was on the African coast may be left to the imagination.' Even the 6d. duty had been absorbed during the period of war-time enforcement in 1760 and 1761. The view has been forcibly expressed that, 'the whole history of the distilling industry in America down to the present day provides evidence of the ability of the industry to prosper while paying excises infinitely greater than that set by the Molasses Act'.* In any case British Treasury officials had good reason to believe that a large proportion of the 3d. duty on molasses would fall not on the British colonists but upon the French West India planters. These, having 'no other method of disposing of them, would be forced to pay the duty and not the people of the colonies', whose lowered purchase prices they would perforce have to accept.† Although this was a revenue measure, it was also a stroke of economic warfare against the remains of the French empire in the Caribbean.

Administrative provisions of the Sugar Act, coupled with the steps already taken to enforce customs regulations, caused considerable hardship and inconvenience in the mainland colonies. All vessels sailing from one colony to another or even crossing the open sea more than seven miles from shore between two places within the same colony, were henceforth required to have clearance papers provided by the nearest customs office. The keenness of the naval officers now acting as ancillaries of the customs service made neglect of this regulation ruinous; for by other clauses of the Act, wherein administrative zeal far outran political discretion and proper concern for the rights of the subject, in cases of seizure onus of proof was put upon the owner, not the customs officer, and officials

---

*L. H. Gipson, *The Coming of the Revolution, 1763–1775* (1954), p. 63.

†*The Jenkinson Papers, 1760–1766*, ed. Ninetta S. Jucker (1949), pp. 346–47.

were given a large degree of protection against prosecution for damages. In consequence coastal traffic which, in truth, the Act had never been intended to touch, was seriously impeded. The masters of small river boats or coasters could not 'take in a few staves, or pig iron, or bar iron, or tar, etc., but they must go thirty or forty miles or more to give bond, the charge for which and his travelling, make the burthen intolerable.'* By the time the government produced an amending act in 1765, to exclude small open vessels of under twenty tons from the obligation to obtain clearance, much avoidable ill-will had been generated.

In the eyes of posterity the administrative shortcoming of Grenville's revenue legislation of 1764 may well loom larger than those alleged at the time in connection with its fiscal provisions. The colonists anticipated greater damage to commerce from these than was in fact probable. Just at this time their apprehensions and difficulties were increased by two other circumstances. One was the government's determination to grasp the nettle of colonial inflation. A statute of 1764 extended to all the colonies a prohibition of the issue of paper money as legal tender which had been imposed upon New England in 1751. Here the ministry tried to grapple more broadly with problems already pin-pointed by the controversy over the Virginia Two-penny Act.† It was concerned to ensure that British merchants did not suffer by having their debts paid in a depreciating currency. Owing to the lack in many colonies of adequate mediums of exchange, this Act helped to cause a trade recession just at the moment when post-war conditions had produced a severe though temporary depression. The timing of this legislation could hardly have been less fortunate, and suffering merchants heaped indiscriminate blame upon all Grenville's measures. Seeking every possible lever against the government, they were in a stronger position than their fellow-subjects at home who resented the cider tax: they could plausibly add to their other arguments the cry of 'no taxation without representation' already raised against the Molasses Act thirty years before. The assemblies of New York

---

*Cited in E. S. and H. M. Morgan, *The Stamp Act Crisis* (new edn., N.Y., 1963), p. 46. See also O. M. Dickerson, *The Navigation Acts and the American Revolution* (Phil., London, 1951), pp. 180–92.

†See pages 28–30 above.

and of North Carolina both protested against the Sugar Act on this ground. Other colonies took it up in advancing objections to the further measure which it was known the government had in view – a colonial stamp tax. In speeches and in pamphlets colonial leaders began to assert the complete fiscal and legislative independence of the colonies in all matters of internal polity.

Despite these alarms Grenville proceeded with the second of his major measures of colonial taxation, the Stamp Act of 1765. The idea was by no means new; a colonial tax of this kind had been suggested on a number of occasions, especially since the commencement of the recent war. In 1764 Grenville obtained preliminary parliamentary approval of his plan among the resolutions which formed the basis of the Sugar Act, but he needed further information before it could be put into effect. To his mind the Sugar Act and a stamp tax were complementary parts of a general fiscal programme designed to meet the needs of the post-war Empire. He clearly underestimated the importance of the difference between the two measures. Whereas the Sugar Act adapted an existing, long-accepted system to new purposes, converting laws for the control of trade into laws for the production of revenue, a stamp act was far more openly an innovation, an imposition of internal taxation upon the colonists by the authority of the imperial parliament.

Grenville regarded his proposal as constitutionally unassailable. Introducing it in the Commons in 1764 he declared that 'he hoped that the power and sovereignty of parliament over every part of the British dominions, for the purpose of raising or collecting any tax, would never be disputed. If there was a single man doubted it he would take the sense of the House, having heard without doors hints of that nature dropped.'* His words were in tune with the views then held by practically all the men in public life in Britain. No-one rose to his challenge. In all the subsequent controversy about stamp taxes the House of Commons went forward in the conviction that it was acting within its constitutional rights and must affirm them. In case of need Grenville had had more detailed arguments prepared by his departmental experts. According to these, American arguments of 'no taxation without represen-

*Cited, Morgan, *The Stamp Act Crisis* (N.Y., 1963), p. 76 and n. 3.

tation' were untenable, for the imperial parliament was not a collection of delegates representing particular places; on the contrary it was the body representative of the dominions of the Crown of Great Britain at large. Tested against political realities this assertion rings hollow, but it had just the sort of legal and logical plausibility which Grenville and most of his contemporaries found unanswerable. Apart from this, so argued Grenville's experts, taxation of the colonies for revenue was already a matter of long-established precedent. Leading instances were the establishment of the American post office by an Act of Queen Anne, the Greenwich Hospital Act of 1729, and the Molasses Act of 1733. They also maintained, evading one of the central points at issue, that the proposed stamp tax would not subvert the powers of the colonial assemblies, since the object to which it was directed, the common defence of the American provinces, lay outside the scope of their activities.*

During the spring of 1764 there seems to have been some fluctuation in Grenville's intentions about American taxation. Obscurities in the evidence have given rise to the view that he deliberately made misleading statements to colonial agents with the idea of blunting colonial opposition, by declaring that no parliamentary tax would be imposed if the colonists would undertake to produce the money in some other way. The agents for Virginia and Massachusetts reported him in this sense. Against this it has been suggested that Grenville carelessly made statements capable of ambiguous interpretation, really meaning that if the colonies could suggest preferable satisfactory alternatives to a stamp tax which he could incorporate into his intended bill he would be glad to hear of them.† Neither of these explanations seems inherently more plausible than a third, that in the spring of 1764 Grenville was willing to try the possibility that the colonial assemblies might make a clear declaration of intent to tax themselves for defence, a course of action which in mid-June the

---

*British Museum, Add. MSS. 38339, fos. 131–5, cited in summary, C. R. Ritcheson, 'The preparation of the Stamp Act', *William and Mary Quarterly*, 3rd s. X (1953), pp. 555–57.

†For the controversy over Grenville's intentions, see Ritcheson, *loc. cit.* pp. 543–59 and E. S. Morgan, 'The postponement of the Stamp Act', *ibid.*, 3 s. VII (1950), pp. 353–92.

Massachusetts assembly rejected. Consistent with this view is the circumstance that no detailed preparations of a stamp bill were set on foot until the summer.

It also seems likely that Grenville sought, as an alternative, the prior consent of the colonial assemblies to a parliamentary stamp bill. This step might obviate constitutional objections which were beginning to be raised in anticipation of the bill (though he himself in any case did not admit their validity). An inspired statement in the Pennsylvania press advocated such a course and upon this ground: by assenting in this way the assemblies would 'avoid every appearance of an infringement of their liberty, and shew their inclination to pay obedience to a British Parliament, which has the power to make every part of the dominions submit to such laws as they may think proper to enact'. Also, by this mode of action, they would prevent 'a precedent from internal taxes being imposed without their consent.* If Grenville indeed had this plan in mind, it was not a reasonable one and indicated his lack of political sensitivity. It involved the colonial assemblies giving prior consent to a revenue measure, whereof the rates, the incidence, and all features save the essential nature of the tax, remained unfixed and unspecified. To have consented on such terms would have required exceptional trust on the part of the colonists.

Preparations were pushed ahead in the autumn of 1764 and in March 1765 the Stamp Act was duly enacted. Colonial complaints were brushed aside and Grenville rejected requests submitted through the colonial agents for a return to the traditional system of requisitions. In the House of Commons opposition to the measure was slight. Grenville introduced his bill on 6th February, and throughout the proceedings upon it the only moment of high tension recorded was during this first debate, when a sharp clash took place between Charles Townshend and Isaac Barré. Townshend defended the bill on its reasonableness: 'And now will these Americans, children planted by our care, nourished up by our indulgence untill they are grown to a degree of strength and opulence, and protected by our arms, will they grudge to contribute their mite to relieve us from the heavy weight of that burden which we lie under.' Barré, who had seen service and made many friends

*Cited, Gipson, *The Coming of the Revolution, 1763-1775* (1954), p. 71.

in America during the late war, denied him point by point:
'They planted by your care? No! Your oppression planted
them in America. . . . They nourished up by your indulgence?
They grew up by your neglect of them. . . . They protected by
your arms? They have nobly taken up arms in your defence.'
As with most rhetorical outbursts there was both truth and
falsehood in his statements; but a deeper understanding of
the American situation than was shared by most members of
parliament rang in the warnings with which he drew his
peroration to a close: 'Believe me, remember I this day told
you so, that same spirit of freedom which actuated that people
at first, will accompany them still. . . . The people, I believe,
are as truly loyal as any subjects the king has, but a people
jealous of their liberties and who will vindicate them, if ever
they should be violated.' A witness of this occasion reported
that 'the whole House sat awhile as amazed, intently looking
and without answering a word'; but less than fifty members
voted against the bill, and there were no further divisions
during its passage in either House.*

The Stamp Act laid duties on documents required in court
proceedings; on instruments of appointment to public office
and licences to practise in the legal profession; on bills of
lading and the papers used in the clearance of ships from
harbour; on a wide range of documents required for commerce
and for transactions in land; on liquor licences, playing cards
and dice, pamphlets and newspapers, and newspaper adver-
tisements. In general the rates of duty were moderate, being
for the most part lighter than the equivalent taxes in Britain.
The anticipated annual yield was about £60,000. As a fiscal
burden they could hardly be described as oppressive. The
funds collected were to be used in America: treasury officials
took considerable pains to explain to American correspondents, that there would be no draining of specie out of the
colonies.

With this enactment the comprehensive overhaul of the
imperial system into which the government had been led in
consequence of the French war was at last complete. Administration of the conquered territories had been provided. A
plan for the wilderness had been adopted which would, it was

*Cited, E. S. Morgan, ed., *Prologue to Revolution. Sources and documents
on the Stamp Act Crisis, 1764–1766* (Chapel Hill, 1959), p. 32.

hoped, combine commercial advantage with the minimum of friction between British and Indians. The commercial system had been tightened up and revised. Military dispositions had been made to meet the increased needs of defence, and to provide also for the policing of the interior. A share of the greatly swollen costs of defence was imposed upon the colonists, partly by the stamp taxes, partly by revenue duties under the Sugar Act, partly by the Quartering Act of 1764 which imposed certain obligations to provide accommodation and supplies for troops; and the new administrative services thus made necessary were partly financed by a further Act of 1765 giving statutory sanction to a system of fees for the services performed by customs officers in issuing clearances and other documents – this was, in effect, a further business tax, to provide payment for the tax-collectors, which was greatly resented by the shipping interests. Even so, the imperial parliament remained responsible for finding more than half the total cost of colonial military defence, its gross liability after 1763 being a good deal greater than it had been when it had defrayed the whole of the much more modest defence costs of the period before 1754. All the various provisions of the years 1763 to 1765 made up a logical, interlocking system. Its one fatal flaw was that it lacked the essential basis of colonial consent.

The Grenville administration was not fated to grapple with the imperial crisis provoked by its measures. Before news of the American reaction reached Britain the chief members of it had ceased to be in office. Their fall had nothing to do with the colonial question. It was due to a deterioration in their personal relations with George III. In the early summer of 1765 the young king at last found deliverance through his uncle, the Duke of Cumberland, from men with whom he was by then on the coldest of terms; and it fell to the youthful and inexperienced members of the Rockingham administration, formed under Cumberland's patronage, to face the American colonists' defiance of the Stamp Act.

CHAPTER FOUR

Authority and the Claims of Liberty, 1765-1770

THE risk involved by an imperial authority acting upon its interpretation of powers instead of within the limits of consensus has seldom been more amply demonstrated than by the events in America in the second half of 1765. The colonists lost little time in defining their position, and words were soon followed by deeds. The Stamp Act gave provocation to all the most influential and vocal sections of colonial society: planters, merchants, lawyers, and printer-publishers. Even elements later committed to loyalism were aligned against it. The activity of the printers and lawyers explains both the rapidity with which the spirit of resistance spread through the colonies and the legalistic nature and intellectual quality of the colonial counter-attack.

As yet American feeling set limits to defiance of imperial authority and opinions about its extent varied considerably. Hardly anyone so far denied the right of Parliament to control imperial matters, especially commerce. There is much evidence to suggest that many colonists, although quite clearly opposed to the Stamp Act on grounds of constitutional principle, were prepared to admit the validity of the Sugar Act.* But in the successive resolutions of the colonial assemblies, in which no distinction between direct and indirect taxes was drawn, a growing opposition to parliamentary taxation of any kind was evident.† As early as 1764 the New York assembly classed both forms alike as inadmissible in its petition against the Sugar Act

*L. H. Gipson, *The British Empire before the American Revolution*, X, pp. 231–40.
†For the illustrative material which follows, see *Prologue to Revolution. Sources and documents on the Stamp Act Crisis, 1764–1766*, ed. by Edmund S. Morgan (Chapel Hill, 1959); and for full treatment of the subject, Edmund S. Morgan and Helen M. Morgan, *The Stamp Act Crisis* (new edn. N.Y. 1963).

and the proposed stamp taxes: 'Since all impositions, whether they be internal taxes, or duties paid for what we consume, equally diminish the estates upon which they are charged: what avails it to any people, by which of them they are impoverished? . . . The whole wealth of a country may be as effectually drawn off, by the exaction of duties, as by another tax upon their estates.' Similarly the Virginian assembly asserted the province's 'right of being governed by such laws respecting their internal polity and taxation as [were] derived from their own consent', and declared they could not discern 'by what distinction they can be deprived of that sacred birthright and most valuable inheritance by their fellow-subjects, nor with what propriety they can be taxed or affected in their estates by the Parliament, wherein they are not, and indeed cannot, constitutionally be represented'. The governor and assembly of Rhode Island stated the case against the Stamp Bill in still more forthright terms,* declaring it would be 'a manifest violation of their just and long enjoyed rights. For it must be confessed by all men, that they who are taxed at pleasure by others, cannot possibly have any property, can have nothing to be called their own; they who have no property can have no freedom, but are indeed reduced to the most abject slavery.'

At the end of May 1765 a group of young zealots in the Virginian House of Burgesses forced through a series of resolves against the Stamp Act. Exaggerated reports, spread by the colonial press, encouraged the other assemblies during the following months to pass sets of resolutions stating with ever-increasing elaboration the grounds for resistance to it. Through all of them ran the claims, that the colonists enjoyed of right all the liberties and privileges of Englishmen, that these rights included freedom from taxation save by their representatives, and that in America the assemblies were the only authorities with lawful powers of taxation. In Rhode Island openly, in New Jersey implicitly, the resolutions indicated that local officials should treat any taxing statute as void. As one assembly after another expressed its reactions, increasing notice was taken of other grievances, notably the use of the vice-admiralty courts.

*Cited in Edmund S. Morgan, 'Colonial Ideas of Parliamentary Power, 1764–66', *William and Mary Quarterly*, 3rd. s., V (1948), pp. 315–17.

In October 1765 delegates from a number of colonies met at New York in the so-called 'Stamp Act Congress'. They passed resolutions reaffirming these points, drew attention also to commercial grievances arising out of the Act of 1764, and petitioned the King and the two Houses of Parliament for relief. They admitted that the colonies owed a 'due subordination' to Parliament, but they rejected outright the view that parliamentary powers included taxation, and they queried, 'whether there be not a material distinction in reason and sound policy, at least, between the necessary exercise of parliamentary jurisdiction in general Acts, for the amendment of the Common Law and the regulation of trade and commerce throughout the whole empire, and the exercise of that jurisdiction by imposing taxes on the colonies'. Meanwhile in newspapers and pamphlets, unchecked by official reticence, detailed and critical arguments about the nature and limits of parliamentary powers were laid before the colonial public.

With the cry 'no taxation without representation' the colonists took firm ground. To Englishmen too this principle was the shield of liberty. Nevertheless the issue was not so clear as this slogan appeared to make it. For what was representation? And what was the real status of Parliament? British politicians and publicists at first attempted to justify the government's policy by maintaining that the colonists were 'virtually' represented in Parliament in the same way as the great majority of men in Britain who had no parliamentary voting rights. The essence of the concept of 'virtual representation' is, that although citizen A does not have the vote, his interests are similar to those of citizen B who does have the vote. Therefore, as a consequence of B's use of his vote, A's interests will receive consideration in the legislature. If B will not tolerate excessive taxes being imposed upon himself and uses his rights as an elector to prevent it, A also is safe from this threat. Such a system may work if there is a close community of interest between all the members of a given political society. The argument wears incredibly thin if A and B are separated by three thousand miles of ocean, and colonial pamphleteers had little difficulty in refuting it.* British politicians were thus

*Leading publications on either side of this argument were *The Regulations Lately Made concerning the Colonies and Taxes Imposed upon them, considered* (1765), by Grenville's secretary to the Treasury, Thomas Whateley; and thrust back into reliance upon the principle of the over-riding supremacy of Parliament throughout all the King's dominions. Historically and intellectually this was satisfactory for them, but it provided no key to the political problem, for it merely opposed an incompatible but equally valid constitutional principle to that put forward by the colonists.

The colonists did not rely merely on argument. With them to think was to act. Initial protests took the form of agreements not to import British goods and to suspend payment of debts to British merchants till such time as the Stamp Act should be repealed. But from the first an important minority of leading men in most of the colonies was prepared for more extreme measures. Convinced that Parliament had acted in excess of its powers and was depriving them of their rights, they were intent to insure that by no overt act whatever should the disputed claims of Parliament be recognized, and that in no way should the refusal to acknowledge them be permitted to interfere with the normal conduct of trade or legal business. Once the Stamp Act came into force, it was impossible legally, without the use of stamped paper, for the law courts to function, for ships to be cleared through the customs, or for various other transactions to take place. Either stamp taxes must be paid, or business must stop. Even members of the most respected classes of colonial society would not tolerate this consequence and took, or connived at, action to prevent it. In North Carolina resistance was led by the gentry of Wilmington, who formed for the purpose an association of 'all the principal gentlemen, freeholders, and other inhabitants' of the neighbouring counties. From New York the commander-in-chief in America reported: 'The lawyers are the source from whence the clamors have flowed in every province. In this province nothing publick is transacted without them, and it is to be wished that even the bench was free from blame. The whole body of merchants in general, assembly men, magistrates, have been united in this plan.'*

*21 Dec. 1765, *The Correspondence of General Thomas Gage . . . 1763–1775*, ed. Clarence E. Carter (2 v., New Haven, 1931–3), I, p. 79.

Daniel Dulany, *Considerations on the Propriety of Imposing Taxes in the British Colonies for the purpose of raising a Revenue by Act of Parliament* (Annapolis, 1765).

The 'plan' was intimidation by riot. The technique was used with – literally – devastating effect. Leading officials and supporters of royal authority were victimized by the destruction of their houses and other property and threatened with loss of life should the mobs lay hands upon them. The 'Sons of Liberty' set the pace at Boston and their example soon spread to other provinces. The men designated as distributors of stamps, some of them prominent colonials, were 'induced' to resign, and the one or two who would not were forced to seek refuge on king's ships in the ports. Colonial governors could avert destruction of the consignments of stamps and stamped paper only by having them stored on board ship or in the local forts: there was not the least possibility of peaceful distribution. The next target for the mobs was the staff of customs houses who demurred about clearing ships without stamped documents. The threat was enough, and within a few weeks of the date the Act was scheduled to take effect business was proceeding normally without stamps in all the American ports. Judges, magistrates, advocates and court officials would soon have come under similar pressure, had not the news early in 1766 of the impending repeal of the Act made it unnecessary to coerce them into opening the courts without complying with it. Royal administration in the colonies was shown to be helpless in face of this massive display of public sentiment. Governors could not use the militia to keep order, for many militia-men were themselves implicated and refused to be embodied to deal with the mobs. It was impossible to protect royal officials who proposed to carry out the provisions of the Act or to preserve their property from attack. The governors had less control of law and order than the conspirators. Indeed, a revolutionary situation had developed, a fact all too evident from the flow of reports into Whitehall during the autumn and winter. During December and January, while the repeal of the Stamp Act was still uncertain, district meetings in various parts of the colonies began to issue declarations of intent to resist enforcement of it even by arms. Grenville publicly declared that there existed a state of rebellion and the indications are that had he still been in office he would have tried to suppress resistance by force. But for the accident of George III's dislike and dismissal of him, and his replacement by men of a more cautious and a milder temper, the American war of independence might have begun in 1766.

On coming into office the members of the Rockingham administration had no clearly defined policy towards America: only one of them had opposed the Stamp Act. Having been in no way identified with the policy of colonial taxation they were well-placed to abandon Grenville's line; and as the reports of riot and disobedience multiplied, this was the course they chose. Conciliation, it is reasonable to suppose, reflected the temperament of the party's leaders as well as their convictions. But the evolution of the ministers' policy was affected both by their internal divisions and by the exigencies of the parliamentary situation, especially by the widespread up-surge of indignation in Parliament at the colonial defiance of imperial authority.

Within the ministry there seem to have been three or even four different shades of opinion. General Conway, brought into the cabinet as an associate of William Pitt, was the only member of it who had earlier openly opposed the Stamp Act, on the ground that Parliament was not representative of the colonists and had no right to tax them – a view which, in deference to majority opinion and the need for ministerial unity, he did not press after he accepted office. Rockingham and his friends were inclined to give some satisfaction to the colonists from a mixture of motives. They were ready to agree that the Stamp Act was injurious to the colonists. They disliked violence and held the not unjustified view, that even if a forceful assertion of imperial authority were temporarily successful (in itself doubtful), in the long run it could only breed disastrous consequences. They were probably attracted by the prospect of discrediting Grenville by stressing the unwisdom of his American policy and wiping it off the statute book. More important, perhaps, they faced strong pressure from commercial interests. The colonists' boycott of British manufactures, and their refusal to settle their debts, created a business crisis which led to a series of petitions against the Stamp Act from merchants in London, and in Liverpool, Bristol, and other outports. The policy of repeal would satisfy the wishes and rally the support of the merchants trading with America, upon whom – so it has been estimated* – about a

*O. M. Dickerson, *The Navigation Acts and the American Revolution* (Phil., London, 1951), pp. 193–94.

quarter of the total liabilities imposed by the Stamp Act would have fallen. Such public support was welcome as off-setting, at least to some extent, the narrowness of the basis of party connection on which the ministry rested in the House of Commons. Other sections of the government thought differently. The Attorney-General, Charles Yorke, and his brother, Lord Hardwicke, members of a family with a strong legal tradition, wished to see parliamentary authority re-affirmed and hankered after enforcement of the Act (perhaps with modifications) as a means of asserting it. The ministers' immediate parliamentary following was similarly divided; and members in general were almost uniformly resentful of the colonists' refusal to bow to parliamentary authority. Apart from these divisions there was a further cause of hesitation: William Pitt, upon whose good favour most of the ministers believed the government to depend for survival in the Com-mons, declined until after the New Year to indicate what policies he would approve.

Once the upsurge of commercial opinion against the Stamp Act became apparent, the ministers, to strengthen their hands in Parliament, cultivated the movement and set their friends to work to shape it to the best advantage. Deliberately the petitioners were steered away from the ticklish question of parliamentary powers – a point on which members of the Commons were exceedingly touchy – and exhorted to con-centrate upon the need to reopen the American trade.

At informal ministerial meetings during the Christmas recess one point seems to have gained fairly general acceptance – a simple surrender to colonial defiance was politically imprac-ticable. Some affirmation of the authority of Parliament was essential. Without this members of Parliament, roused by prophecies of impending colonial independence from Grenville and other leaders of opposition, were likely to give an over-whelming majority to proposals for enforcing the Act as it stood in order to teach the colonists their place. The idea of a Declaratory Bill, strongly pushed by Yorke, was thus accepted in principle, only Conway and one other minister opposing it openly, though it seems likely that Rockingham and his immediate circle regarded it as a distasteful necessity. Apart from this, ministers seem to have thought at first not of re-pealing the Act but of making it less burdensome. It was suggested that the charges on ships' cockets and clearances might be greatly reduced; that duties specified in the Act should be paid in local currency instead of sterling; and that the courts of vice-admiralty should be debarred from dealing with prosecutions for violations of it. But there was no clear agreement to act. Divided, the ministers hesitated over what was right and what was practicable, until they had the matter decided for them by William Pitt.

When Parliament reassembled in January 1766 Pitt declared himself for the first time on the American question. In the course of two flaming speeches in which he praised the colonists for their resistance in defence of liberty and distributed blame all round among the British politicians, he demanded that the Stamp Act be repealed 'absolutely, totally, and immediately'. At the same time he confirmed the provisional decision of the ministers in favour of a Declaratory Bill: 'Let the sovereign authority of this country over the colonies be asserted in as strong terms as can be desired, and be made to extend to every point of legislation whatever. That we may bind their trade, confine their manufactures, and exercise every power whatsoever, except that of taking their money out of their pockets without their consent.'*

Rockingham now knew what was to be done if the government was to retain the vitally important support of Pitt in the Commons. But the ministers could not directly follow Pitt's line, for he had raised what would have been a most embarrassing issue. Accepting as valid the distinction drawn by the Stamp Act Congress between taxation as a function of local representation and general regulation as a function of the imperial parliament, he wished the Stamp Act to be repealed on the ground that it had been founded on an erroneous constitutional principle, in contravention of the basic right of 'no taxation without representation'. Hardly any of the ministers (perhaps Conway alone) took this view of the question – nor did private members in the Commons, most of whom believed Parliament to have full powers, and whose opinions had to be respected if the government's legislation was to secure passage. The ministers wished to have as little said about authority as possible. In evading the issue raised by Pitt they were aided by a widespread misunderstanding of what Pitt

* *The Parliamentary History*, xvi, cols. 97–100.

had said. George Grenville and most of Pitt's critics believed that he had drawn a distinction between internal (direct) taxation by the Stamp Act and external (indirect) taxation by the Sugar Act and had held that the second was admissible while the first was not – an error repeated by many historians. In fact Pitt denounced all taxation of the colonists by Parliament but held that this limitation of power did not extend to the imposition of duties framed for the control of trade which might incidentally, but not of intent, produce a revenue. It appears that the ministers did nothing to dispel this confusion in the minds of members of Parliament, because they felt that less emotional reaction would be roused against the policy of yielding the substance of the Stamp Act if it remained. When Benjamin Franklin was brought before the Commons shortly afterwards to testify (in a doubtless carefully rehearsed performance) regarding conditions in America, he helped to foster this erroneous impression with regard to the colonists themselves.*

The same desire to slur over instead of clarifying the constitutional issue led to a deliberate evasiveness in the wording of the Declaratory Bill. A formula was adopted which might be read in one way by the colonists, and by Pitt, and in another by the majority of members of Parliament. The resolution on which the Bill was founded declared, that the British legislature 'had, hath, and of right ought to have, full power and authority to make laws and statutes of sufficient force and validity to bind the colonies and people of America, subjects of the Crown of Great Britain, in all cases whatsoever'. During the drafting a proposal by Yorke to include a mention of taxation was rejected by Rockingham: it would have sacrificed the support of Pitt and it would have been an outright challenge to the colonists. The Bill therefore was capable of being taken to exclude the taxing power, and many colonists so understood it when the text came to be published. But had the ministers interpreted it this way in Parliament, there is little doubt that a majority would have been against it and against the repeal of the Stamp Act for which it was intended to clear the ground. None of them repudiated the view held by most members of the Commons, that the 'power and authority to make laws and statutes' included the taxing power – some

Ibid. cols. 144, 158–9.

of them shared this opinion. In debate many private members specifically attached the wider meaning to these words, but as the House rigidly enforced its rule of secrecy no authoritative report of this fact reached the colonists.

The Declaratory Bill was speeded through the House of Commons without a division, criticized ineffectively only by Pitt and one or two of his friends. In the House of Lords only five peers voted against it on the ground that it made exaggerated claims for Parliament. But there was bitter opposition to the repeal of the Stamp Act. The resolutions for repeal were carried in a crowded House of Commons by 275 votes to 167 and in the Lords after a hard fight by a majority of only 34. The figures indicate the difficulty the ministry would have encountered had they attempted repeal without satisfying members' constitutional scruples by the Declaratory Act. They were walking a parliamentary tight-rope, and this explains an excessive nervousness they showed at the height of the affair regarding the attitude of George III.

Once the alternatives of repeal or enforcement of the Stamp Act were clearly posed, the King accepted repeal. He had no desire to widen the breach between Britain and the colonies. Also he wished to avoid the collapse of the ministry and the return to power of Grenville, whom he hated. But he regretted the abandonment of the proposed modification of the Act, which would have made concessions to the economic but not the constitutional grievances of the colonists. In order to carry waverers in both Houses Rockingham sought and obtained leave to make it generally known that the King personally favoured repeal rather than enforcement. Unwisely the King let fall among the courtiers that he preferred modification to either of these courses. At the same time he declined to sanction the dismissal from minor offices of members of the Earl of Bute's party who were opposed to repeal, for he thought their support in general matters essential to the survival of the ministry. Rockingham and his friends were much concerned. Afterwards they came to feel that they had not been treated with confidence, and that the King had committed a calculated indiscretion in the course of intriguing for their removal and traversing their policy behind their backs; whereas in fact it seems more likely that the King's well-known nervous volubility had betrayed him into an unintentional indiscretion.

Having, as they hoped, settled the main grievance of the colonists, in the following months the ministry pushed through – as a commercial measure – various changes in the Sugar Act of 1764. In place of the threepenny duty on foreign molasses, a flat rate of one penny per gallon was imposed on all molasses, British or foreign, imported into the colonies. Duties charged on British raw sugar entering the mainland colonies were repealed. Import duties payable in the colonies on the entry of East Indian and French textiles were abolished: instead these goods were to pay an export duty when shipped from Great Britain. The government also provided for the opening of free ports in the West Indies, in the hope of reviving the former direct, illicit trade with the Spanish in the Caribbean. This move was expected to renew the inflow of specie which assisted colonial merchants to discharge debts owed in Britain, but it proved a failure. All this legislation showed a willingness to foster colonial trade and modify regulations which had come under criticism. But no step shows more clearly how little instinctive sympathy the members of the Rockingham administration had for the constitutional claims of the colonists than the change in the molasses duty. With all element of preference removed, the duty could not on any pretext be regarded as for the regulation of trade. It was simply a revenue measure, which brought in a substantial yield during the following years. However so low a duty was not felt to be burdensome and no complaint seems to have been raised by the colonists on the ground of principle.

The Stamp Act crisis was over, but its legacy remained. Both in America and in Great Britain the events of 1765–1766 caused a hardening of attitudes and opinions, which persisted throughout the remaining years of the imperial crisis and determined the course which it followed.

The desire to conciliate was most marked among the members of the Rockingham party. Their claim to be the most statesmanlike of the various British political groups in their approach to the imperial problem is indisputable. As the handling of the molasses duty indicates, most of them were convinced of the validity of claims of parliamentary supremacy over the colonies, including the taxing power. But they were also convinced of the need to avoid exercising this supremacy in a provocative fashion: not long afterwards two or three of the leading members of the party were to be found openly admitting that it would be better to suffer the colonists to force a gradual, inevitable loosening of imperial bonds, even to the point of complete independence, rather than bring on a tragic conflict which might destroy British power and prosperity.* More than any other group (except for some of Pitt's friends) they revealed an awareness of colonial strength and of the need to adjust policy to circumstances rather than to adhere rigidly to the historic frame of the constitution. Had not their excessive concern with faction politics prevented them in 1767 from joining forces with other politicians favourably disposed to colonial claims, who were left leaderless in Chatham's ministry as a result of Chatham's mental collapse, events in the next few years might have followed a very different course.†

One consequence of the Declaratory Act they did not foresee: it assigned a greater authority to Parliament than Grenville had originally asserted with the Stamp Act. In Grenville's view Parliament had power to tax the colonists in virtue of its established position as the supreme legislature of the whole Empire and because the colonists were virtually represented. After 1766 the legal fact was established that Parliament had power to tax the colonists by virtue of its own legislative declaration. As a recent writer has observed: 'Repeal of the Stamp Act, unaccompanied by the Declaratory Act, could have been utilized as a demonstration that virtual representation worked.' But after 1766, 'The British government had abandoned the constitutional position which linked them with the Americans and had retreated to the heights of arbitrary declaration.'‡

The stand taken by William Pitt, soon to be Earl of Chatham, reflected the paradoxical nature of that strange mentality. Pitt had rejoiced that America had resisted, shocking his countrymen in the Commons by the appearance of condoning rebellion. He was aware, as he said later, that the colonists must be grasped in the arms of affection. He attempted to defend them by drawing a dubious distinction between taxation and legislation – a distinction which, through the twist

*J. Brooke, *The Chatham Administration, 1766–1768* (1956), pp. 369–74.
†*Ibid.*, p. 332.
‡Morgan, *The Stamp Act Crisis* (2nd edn., N.Y., 1963), pp. 361–62 .

given to it by Grenville and others, contributed to the misleading and dangerous belief that the colonists accepted a
distinction between internal and external taxation. And yet
Pitt demanded the assertion of Parliament's general legislative
powers over the colonies with a vehemence totally alien to the
spirit shown by the Rockingham party. This circumstance –
though it was not the only one – added to the difficulty of
securing co-operation between them later over an effective
policy of conciliation.

Pitt's associate, the Earl of Shelburne, adopted a more
statesmanlike attitude than Pitt. He opposed the Declaratory
Act outright, on the ground that the constitutional relations
between Great Britain and the colonies were better left un-
defined. 'It was unwise,' he declared in Parliament, 'to raise
the question of right.' His viewpoint was thus closer to that
of the Rockinghams; and he was more fortunate than they
because, not being muzzled by office, he had no need to compromise his convictions (as Conway did) to smooth the way
for repeal.

On the other side of the question stood the three factions
led by Grenville, by the Duke of Bedford, and (for a few
months longer only) by the Earl of Bute. Their attitude was
most clearly voiced in debate by Grenville, who several times
declared that the rioting in defiance of the Stamp Act was
simply rebellion and called for appropriate counter-measures.
Both he and his allies of the Bedford party resented the abandonment of their American policy and believed a step fatal
to the Empire had been taken by the failure to assert British
authority in America. Dismissing Pitt's untenable distinction
between taxation and legislation, they maintained that an
admission of inability to tax would also be an admission of
inability to legislate, which must set the colonists 'absolutely
free from any obedience to the power of the British legislature'.
Unable to discern the fundamental unity of the Anglo-
American commercial system, they foretold economic ruin
arising from a colonial rejection of all British commercial
regulation. One surrender to violence would entail a succession of others. Members of all these groups believed in the
rigid maintenance of British authority over the colonies, and
their gradual infiltration back into office (though without
Grenville and Bedford, who both died within the next six

years, or Bute, who finally retired from politics in 1766) boded ill for the internal peace of the empire. Moreover, as colonial bickering on various subordinate issues continued, waverers in the Commons came to share their view that repeal had been a mistake and a sign of weakness.

In the colonies the Rockingham ministry's legislation gave less satisfaction than its authors hoped. At first there was a general feeling of relief. The non-importation agreements were called off and normal trade was resumed. Pitt was mistakenly credited with securing a parliamentary surrender of the right of taxation, and the disappointment when the true state of affairs came to be understood was all the greater.

The leaders of the resistance movement in the colonies were misled less on the whole than the generality of their country-men. They rejoiced in the repeal of the Stamp Act, but they perceived the ambiguities of the Declaratory Act, and they received sufficient hints from correspondents near the centre of British politics to realize that the Act in fact reinforced the claims of Parliament. This knowledge caused them to hold together as far as possible the quasi-revolutionary organiza-tions they had built up during the Stamp Act crisis. More-over, despite strong hints, they continued to give provocation by words if not by deeds. The Rockingham ministry sought to damp down the argument, knowing that continued colonial assertions of their rights would only enrage political opinion in Britain and stiffen the attitude of those politicians who had opposed repeal. Nevertheless, although colonial assemblies voted loyal Addresses of thanks for repeal, they insisted upon reaffirming their own belief that Parliament had no right of taxation in America. After some prevarication they agreed to compensate victims of the Stamp riots; but in Massachusetts this led to a further defiance of British authority, for the legislature insisted upon coupling with the compensation a general pardon and indemnity to those responsible for the riots, and the subsequent disallowance of this act was tacitly ignored.

The events of 1765 and 1766 assured the ascendancy in colonial politics of the outspoken champions of provincial rights. Particularly in the leading colonies of Massachusetts and Virginia, power passed into the hands of the groups which were later to lead the Revolution. Men attached to the royal governments or sympathetic towards them – the American 'Tories' of the revolutionary period – were marked down, pushed out of public life, and their political influence destroyed. Moderate men, who were entirely opposed to Parliament's claims but who would never have contemplated violent resistance, also in many cases lost their influence. Not the least significant result of the crisis was that the peoples of the various provinces, whose disputes and rivalries had been notorious, and who had been able to achieve only a very imperfect unity of effort against the French a decade before, had managed to co-operate in a common cause and had begun to develop a sense of separate common identity in resisting British encroachments on their constitutional rights. Finally, a discussion of these rights had been provoked, and once provoked could not be silenced. By 1765 James Otis was already asking the question, 'why trade, commerce, arts, sciences, and manufactures, should not be as free for an American as for a European?' The logical end of such speculation was the abrogation of the laws of trade. Events were soon to show the importance of these developments.

After 1766 a permanent relaxation of tension between Britain and the colonies depended above all on one main condition – that power should remain in the hands of the Rockinghams or of other moderate men, who were willing not to raise the issue of taxation, and ready to yield if necessary on still wider questions of legislative authority for the sake of harmony within the empire. But within three months of repeal, the parliamentary weakness of the ministry proved fatal. The new government formed by William Pitt, now made Earl of Chatham, lacked talent, depended very largely on his prestige and experience, and was left rudderless by his mental collapse early in 1767. In his absence the lead was taken by his forceful but erratic Chancellor of the Exchequer, Charles Townshend, who speedily provoked a new American crisis.

Recent studies have vividly portrayed the strange, twisted character of this man, whose disastrous lack of judgment now produced a fatal repetition of the recently repudiated policy of Grenville.* Charming, brilliant, rebellious, politically

*Sir Lewis Namier, *Charles Townshend: his character and career* (The Leslie Stephen Lecture, 1959), repr. in his *Crossroads of Power* (1962), pp. 194–212 Sir Lewis Namier and John Brooke, *Charles Townshend* (1964).

insensitive, unstable, he nursed one fixed idea, that the colonial governors and their officials should be assured financial independence from their legislatures by grants of a permanent civil list in each colony. A slave to flattery, instead of invoking statesmanship (which was beyond him) he pandered to the worst emotions of the Commons with a manoeuvre which bore no relation to the problem with which it purported to deal.

Early in 1767, faced in the Commons with discontent at continued high taxation, Townshend waywardly agreed with the chief opposition spokesman, Grenville, that the colonists ought to pay part of the costs of their defence. When it became clear during the following weeks, that the cost of the garrisons in America was running – far above the estimate – at an annual level of some £700,000, he insisted upon the withdrawal of the costly posts in the interior, upon abandonment to the colonies of the expense of Indian relations, and upon a measure of colonial taxation. This last suggestion found additional favour in Parliament because for some months there had been exasperating colonial defiance of a Mutiny Act passed in 1765. The Act imposed obligations to provide billets and supplies, and was rather naturally regarded in the colonies as yet another piece of parliamentary taxation; and the row did not end until after Parliament had passed a statute suspending the legislative activities of the New York legislature until the province should comply.

However Townshend's Revenue Bill was inconsequent alike in its premises and in its provisions – a perfect reflection of the man. Although Townshend thought the distinction between internal and external taxation nonsensical (as it was), he nevertheless seized upon Franklin's testimony the previous year as evidence that the colonists had no objection to revenue duties – a preposterous piece of verbal legerdemain in face of the massive witness to the contrary in colonial resolutions and petitions. Of the commodities which he selected to be charged with duties on importation into the colonies, only tea passed in great quantities and might yield a good revenue. Glass, paints, lead, and paper were not imported on a large scale (and at a pinch could be provided from colonial resources)*:

*O. M. Dickerson, *The Navigation Acts and the American Revolution*, (Phil., London, 1951) p. 196.

goods which were – such as British textiles – he avoided. The money to be raised from the new duties could in all cases have been secured much more cheaply and surely in Britain, by merely retaining excises already paid instead of continuing to allow drawback on exports to the colonies: as Burke later pointed out, in order that Townshend should have his way in subjecting the colonists to parliamentary taxation, the revenue services went through the absurd routine of paying out moneys already in the government's hands as drawback when merchants shipped the goods to the colonies and then collecting it back again (or trying to) when the goods arrived in colonial ports.* Finally, although this piece of colonial taxation had been suggested in connection with military expenditure, Townshend allotted the proceeds to a civil list for colonial governors and other officials. To strengthen the administrative machinery Townshend provided for the establishment of an American Board of Customs at Boston, and he gave further provocation with another (abortive) Act authorizing superior colonial courts to issue writs of assistance.†

The Revenue Act of 1767 posed a far more serious threat to colonial self-government than Grenville's measures. Grenville had specifically disclaimed any intention of reducing the role of the assemblies, and had given an assurance of this by earmarking the stamp revenues for imperial military purposes only. But Townshend was moved by this very intention: he wanted the governors to be unfettered by financial dependence upon their assemblies in their task of executing and enforcing imperial policy. From the colonial viewpoint, if this plan were successful the one lever by which they enforced the will of the province upon the governor would be destroyed. What Parliament had won from the Stuarts would be denied to them. So far as they were concerned, the constitutional progress of the last hundred years (which conformed with the British pattern) would be reversed. Their legislatures might, by British tolerance, retain some share in provincial government, but it would be precarious and by suffrance, not inherent and enforceable. It is a measure of the confusion, weakness, and lack of political insight of even the large and, by dignity of office,

* *The Parliamentary History,* xvii, col. 1224.

†On writs of assistance see p. 37 above. The hostility of public opinion in the colonies made the measure nugatory.

preponderant pro-American section in the cabinet, that they failed to see the dangers of Townshend's policy and resist it even to the point of forcing him to resign.*

In the colonies the reaction to the Townshend Act repeated, and in some respects surpassed, the defiance of the Stamp Act two years before. At the first news of it the merchants and radical leaders sought to repeat their pressure campaign against British merchants and politicians and combined to organize a non-consumption agreement directed against all imports from Great Britain. Within a few months this was supplemented by a second non-importation agreement, to which the general bodies of merchants in all the main colonial commercial centres had given adherence by the beginning of 1769. Much of the responsibility for this success was due to the radical Boston lawyer, Samuel Adams, whose faction was now firmly in control of Boston politics. In January 1768, at his instigation, the Massachusetts House of Representatives remonstrated strongly in a petition to the King and in letters to leading British politicians. In February it approved the circulation to other colonial legislatures of a manifesto, drafted by Adams, which denounced the Townshend duties as violating the principle of no 'taxation without representation', attacked the proposed colonial civil list as unconstitutional, rejected the idea of colonial representation at Westminster, sketched the plans for resistance at Boston, and called for joint action in defence of colonial liberties. British efforts to frustrate its favourable reception in other provinces merely increased ill feeling. Virginia and several other colonies gave it their hearty assent. Intellectual justifications for the stand against the Act poured from the colonial press, notably in John Dickinson's *Letters from a Farmer in Pennsylvania*, in which the author argued against Parliament's right to impose any 'commercial regulation' for the purpose of raising revenue.

As in 1765, the colonial reaction soon developed into something more than a merely passive boycott of British goods. Organized resistance prevented effective interference with smuggling, and acts of violence – including the occasional tarring and feathering of customs officials – reduced royal

*Conway and Shelburne, secretaries of state; Grafton, First Lord of the Treasury; Camden, Lord Chancellor. See the discussion of this question in Namier and Brooke, *Charles Townshend*, pp. 172–79.

administration to a nullity. The law-courts were powerless. In plain face of the evidence juries refused to convict. So rarely could a prosecution be mounted, that the four new vice-admiralty courts set up in 1768 with judges paid on the home establishment made no contribution to the restoration of imperial authority. In the spring of 1768 the newly established American Board of Customs was terrorized into withdrawing from Boston to the safety, first, of a warship, and then of the fortress of Castle William.

At Boston the resoluteness of one or two big trading houses closely connected with the lieutenant-governor resulted in fairly large-scale defiance of the non-importation agreement, but elsewhere the boycott, aimed particularly at tea, had almost complete success. There were ominous developments at New York and Philadelphia. Local merchant houses established regular trade connections in Holland, contrary to the Navigation Acts and the Acts of Trade. Dutch tea was openly imported illegally in vast quantities and new lucrative channels of export trade were established. Other illicit commerce was opened through the Dutch West India island entrepôt of St. Eustatius and through the Portuguese Atlantic islands. New England patriots were forced into a search for local substitutes, but in the middle and southern colonies tea-drinking was hardly interrupted. British imperial authority and the system of commercial regulation – which really rested on a basis, not of force, but of consent and mutual convenience – collapsed like a house of cards. Having once burst these bounds Quakers and New Yorkers showed no willingness to retreat back within them when the non-importation agreement was called off late in 1770. Ominous for the future was the degree of support for resistance among men who, two years before, had been opposed to the organized violence against the Stamp Act. This new provocation had further eroded respect for law and the traditional authority of the British government, and in London the direst prophecies of the opponents of conciliation seemed the more justified.

By the end of 1768 it had become clear in London that, short of military enforcement, no appreciable revenue was to be expected from the Townshend duties. However, governing circles still shrank from such extremes. Troops were sent to Boston to maintain order but no attempt was made to use them for purposes of coercion. Early in 1769 stern measures were proposed by Lord Hillsborough, then secretary of state for the colonies.* He suggested that the Massachusetts charter should be amended, so that the council should become nominated instead of elective, as in the other royal governments; and that, by the same statute, it should be enacted that any further resolution of the assembly denying or questioning Parliament's authority should automatically cancel the charter. George III himself, in one of his rarely-recorded interventions in policy-making, opposed these suggestions, observing that the altering of charters was 'at all times an odious measure', and that the second proposal seemed rather 'calculated to increase the unhappy feuds that subsist than to assuage them'. The other ministers were of his mind and chose retreat. In the spring of 1769 it was agreed in principle to abolish all the Townshend duties except that on tea. No concession was made to colonial argument. The measure was justified on the ground that taxation of articles of British manufacture was contrary to the true principles of commerce. Legislation to this effect was passed early in 1770.

In 1770 the government retained the tea duty as a symbol of Parliament's legislative and taxing powers over the colonies. Nearly half the cabinet thought the attempt to save the point ill-judged, and the decision was carried by a majority of five to four only. From a fiscal or commercial point of view the duty was of little significance on either side of the Atlantic, but henceforth it stood as a fatal stumbling-block to the restoration of good relations between Great Britain and the colonies. In Britain there was no willingness to repeal unless a clear admission of subordination was first offered by the colonists by giving obedience to it. A majority of the colonial politicians, angry and suspicious, and intent on not compromising the principle of no 'taxation without representation,' refused to consider this concession.

---

*Early in 1768 a third secretaryship of state was set up with responsibility for the colonies. The holders of this office were Lord Hillsborough (1768–72), the Earl of Dartmouth (1772–75), Lord George Germain (1775–82), and Welbore Ellis (Feb.–March 1782). In March 1782 the office was discontinued.

CHAPTER FIVE

Confrontation, 1770-1774

THE modification of the Revenue Act in 1770 produced, by the beginning of 1771, the breakdown of the colonial non-consumption and non-importation agreements and the restoration to a large extent of normal trade. The legacy of distrust kindled in the minds of colonial politicians by the Act and by the retention of the tea duty was not so easily expunged. Many circumstances, some general, some confined to particular colonies, tended to perpetuate it.

At Boston hatred of the customs officials was deeply ingrained, despite an improvement in their conduct after 1770. The dissolution of the assembly after its approval of the circular against the Townshend Act was regarded as a blow at constitutional liberty; and a still greater menace was felt from the presence of the British garrison (until it was withdrawn to Castle William after the 'Boston Massacre').*

In the southern colonies especially, there was continued resentment of the Currency Act of 1764 and annoyance at the government's rejection of a number of petitions for leave to issue currency bills of legal tender. Although certain colonies had in the past undoubtedly abused the practice of issuing bills of credit the Act created real difficulties owing to the lack of a sufficient medium of exchange. Various assemblies attempted to overcome the currency difficulties of their provinces by issuing bills which, though not full legal tender, were declared to be so for the purpose of local taxation, but they encountered what seemed an arbitrary opposition from Whitehall, some acts being disallowed while others were not. Not until 1773 did the government accept the necessity for some such arrangement. In the meantime, as local trade was hampered by lack of a local currency, its image was tarnished with an impression of indifference to colonial needs and interests.

Irritation also grew in the south over the Crown's insistence

*For the 'Boston Massacre' see p. 77 below.

75

on its prerogative in various constitutional matters. In 1767 a general instruction went out to all colonial governors, to resist the assemblies' encroachments with regard to the erection of new constituencies, the apportionment of representation, the fixing of qualifications for electors and representatives, the holding of sessions, or the duration of the legislature. Some of these were issues which the westward expansion of the colonies was making acute. In South Carolina there were stormy passages between the assembly and the royal officials over bills to set up new courts in outlying districts, with judges appointed during good behaviour. An irreconcilable quarrel also developed over the assembly's grant of £1,500 to the Bill of Rights Society in London for supporting the American cause along with that of John Wilkes. The governor refused to let it continue in session unless it would purge its error, and from 1771 its activities were in abeyance. Relations between the governors and the assemblies in North Carolina and in Georgia were marred by a series of disputes over jurisdiction concerning non-resident debtors, the appointment of colonial agents, and the regulation of office fees.*

Continued friction involved continuing criticism of the various institutionalized forms of British control. This in its turn provoked a process of rationalization of colonial claims, in consequence of which they became step by step more extreme. The consequences were to be seen in the attitudes both of individuals and of groups. At one extreme Samuel Adams of Boston, as early as 1768, was preaching armed resistance in anticipation of the threatened arrival of British troops. Washington, not yet a commanding figure in Virginian politics, though much more moderate than Adams, recorded in 1769 his view, that the British government seemed intent on hedging in American liberties and that these might have to be defended by force of arms. Benjamin Franklin, the most illustrious and famous American of his day, criticizing in 1770 the retention of the tea duty and the stationing of troops in Boston without the consent of the Massachusetts assembly, expressed the view, that the American provinces were 'so

*An excellent general account of these causes of friction in the southern colonies is in Jack P. Greene, *The Quest for Power. The Lower Houses of Assembly in the Southern Royal Colonies, 1689–1776* (Chapel Hill, N.C., 1963), pp. 380–437.

many distinct and separate states', and that 'our having the same Head or Sovereign, the King, will not justify such an invasion of the separate right of each state to be consulted on the establishment of whatever force is proposed to be kept within its limits, and to give or refuse its consent, as shall appear most for the public good of that state'. Parliament, Franklin declared, 'had usurped an authority of making laws for them, which before it had not'.* In similar vein the Massachusetts assembly resolved in mid-1769: 'That this House do concur in and adhere to . . . that essential principle, that no man can be taxed, or bound in conscience to obey any law, to which he has not given his consent in person or by his representative.'† Although this resolution was afterwards watered down, the original text was given wide publicity in the colonial press. In 1770 the party of resistance in Boston provoked a series of incidents with the military, which led finally to the death of five persons in the fraças known as the 'Boston Massacre' – a course of action which succeeded in its object of forcing the withdrawal of the troops to the island fort of Castle William.‡ The 'Massacre' provided the emotional impetus for a series of vehement resolutions at a Boston town meeting, including a protest against the pretended right or power, 'of any exterior authority upon earth, to determine, limit or ascertain all or any of our constitutional or chartered, natural, or civil, political, or sacred, rights, liberties, privileges or immunities.'§

The Townshend duties, the military occupation, and the 'Massacre', all skilfully exploited by the talented propagandist, Samuel Adams, totally destroyed the hitherto fairly amicable relations which had subsisted between the governor and the Massachusetts legislature. Both the council and the assembly came to be dominated by the party of resistance. Shifts adopted in the hopes of strengthening the royal government, which had become virtually inoperative in face of popular opposition, merely embittered the conflict. When the governor assumed he

*A. H. Smyth (ed.), *The writings of Benjamin Franklin* (10 v., N.Y., 1907), pp. 259–60.

†Cited in Gipson, *The Coming of the Revolution, 1763–1775* (1954), p. 199.

‡On this episode see John C. Miller, *Sam Adams, Pioneer in Propaganda* (Boston, 1936), pp. 167–88.

§Cited in Gipson, *The Coming of the Revolution, 1763–1775* (1954), p. 203.

had authority to convene the assembly at Cambridge instead
of at Boston, in the belief that it would be less under mob
influence, the members for many months refused to do business
at all. The council declined to give executive sanction to any
proposed administrative action by the governor in support
of controversial parliamentary enactments. The home government's decision to pay the governor's salary out of funds
supplied from Britain, giving him financial independence
from the assembly, aroused a series of rumbling protests, and
these were fanned into a flame when it became known in
1772, that judges' salaries were to be similarly provided.
Dialogue between the governor and the assembly disclosed a
complete divergence of views about the location and extent
of constitutional authority within the Empire. The governor
declared he knew –

no line that can be drawn between the supreme authority of parliament and the total independence of the colonies. It is impossible that
there should be two independent legislatures in one and the same
state, for although there may be but one head, the King, yet two
legislative bodies will make two governments as distinct as the
Kingdoms of England and Scotland before the Union.

For the governor, posing the issue this way, the denial to the
provincial legislatures of equality with Parliament was an
essential attribute of empire: without this the empire would
not exist. But the assembly believed such equality essential to
freedom. Its answer, drawn up by Samuel Adam's ally, John
Adams, was uncompromising:

If there be no such line, the consequence is, either that the colonies
are vassals of the parliament, or that they are totally independent.
As it cannot be supposed to have been the intention of the parties
in the compact, that we should be reduced to a state of vassalage,
the conclusion is, that it was their sense, that we were thus independent.

Thus in Massachusetts, especially, the insistence on each side
upon constitutional rights helped to frustrate moves towards
compromise and pushed the colonists towards the assertion of
claims of statehood.* At the instigation of the radicals the
legislature began to adopt terms which implied this status.

*For this exchange, *ibid.*, pp. 212–13.

The assembly called itself 'His Majesty's Commons' instead of 'The House of Representatives of Massachusetts', its meeting-place the 'State House' instead of the 'Court House', and reports of its proceedings were referred to as parliamentary debates.

Equally indicative of the underlying seriousness of the crisis in imperial relations was the growing disregard of the laws of navigation and trade and of the remaining revenue law imposing a duty on tea. Despite the ending of the non-importation agreement, only a negligible amount of British tea was imported into either New York or Philadelphia. The great consumption in the middle and southern colonies continued to depend upon illegal importation from Holland or via other routes opened up after 1767. Though fairly large amounts of dutied tea came into Boston, large-scale smuggling continued in all the New England colonies. In face of connivance by local authorities, of violent resistance, and of ruthless harassment by actions for damages in the local civil courts, the customs and preventive officers were helpless. When in 1772 a revenue vessel, which had run aground near Providence, Rhode Island, was seized and burnt, it proved impossible to trace the culprits. Resistance to revenue officers had become a public duty. Smuggling and violence went on, tolerated and often connived at by those sober elements of society who, in normal times, would have been the natural upholders of law and order. The would-be legitimate trader was harassed and on occasion forced out of business by local committees of patriots, who, in places like Boston, were gradually assuming the position of a state within a state.

While Massachusetts set the pace in resistance during the early 1770s, the Boston radicals took great care to publicize their case throughout the colonies and to insist that they were the champions of a common cause. Of such propaganda campaigns Samuel Adams and his associates were now past-masters. Nor were their pleas unheeded. When in 1772 the Boston town meeting protested vigorously against the payment of judges from imperial funds and formed a committee of correspondence to bring its grievances to the notice of the other provinces, the example of a standing committee was quickly adopted by the Virginia assembly, at the instigation of future revolutionary leaders such as Patrick Henry and

Thomas Jefferson, and other colonies soon followed suit. Not only were the colonies beginning to feel their statehood, but under the pressure of the dispute with the imperial government, the leaders in various provinces were coming to feel that sense of common concern which makes, and marks, a nation.

This incipient but ominous development did not escape the attention of the ministers. Again and again the dispatches of colonial governors echoed the refrain that the colonists were aiming at independence. It is doubtful if by 1772 such an object had been consciously formulated by any save a few extremists. But colonial demands now clearly amounted to a large measure of autonomy. To governing circles in London this seemed incompatible with a continuance of the protectionist imperial commercial system, without which, they believed, Great Britain could not sustain the wealth and status of an independent Great Power. This underlying fear of political and economic ruin was the primary consideration drawing the British government on into the final disaster of the American Revolution. There were important contributory factors, misunderstandings in part attributable to the sheer distance separating the colonies from the mother country, so that it was easy to misread strategic signposts as the tale of incidents unfolded. Mistakenly reassured by the governors about the loyalty of the propertied classes in the colonies, the ministers underestimated the spirit of American resistance. From the collapse of Samuel Adams's bluster about armed resistance at Boston they drew the conclusion that the colonists would always bow to a show of force. On the reports of officers who had served during the French war they underrated the fighting power of the untrained and discipline-hating colonist. Finally, they believed that Massachusetts was more isolated in its radical stand than was in fact the case. The misconceptions were not all on one side. The colonists argued from past British hesitations and reversals of policy that a show of resistance would always make them back down; and many years of newspaper propaganda, into which much prejudice, falsehood, misunderstanding, and sheer ignorance had been loaded, had spread a totally misleading impression of political, social and personal decadence and collapse in Great Britain.*

*See, for example, John C. Miller, *Sam Adams. Pioneer in Propaganda* (Boston, 1936), pp. 145-7.

In the spring of 1773 the question, what was to be done about Massachusetts, was already under contemplation by the government. But it was a measure of a quite different kind which, at the end of that year, brought on the final breach within the empire. The occasion was a crisis in the financial affairs of the East India Company.

In May 1773 the ministry piloted through Parliament a Tea Act which gave extensive advantages and privileges to the Company. In order to facilitate sale of enormous surpluses of tea lying in the Company's London warehouses, all duties charged on tea on re-export were remitted, and the Company was also authorized to set up its own retail agencies in the colonies. It was considered that the remission of duty would permit so great a reduction in the price of tea, that the vent in America would be greatly increased and that smuggled Dutch tea would be beaten out of the market. The main object was to assist the Company. There is no doubt that, at the same time, the ministers expected that the new arrangement would lead to a much more general acceptance in America of the colonial import duty on tea left in force by the Act of 1770. In the course of debate they rejected outright opposition proposals that the Townshend duty should be repealed as a conciliatory gesture to the colonists and some part of the drawback retained instead: it was rumoured afterwards, that the Company had offered to pay an export duty of twice the colonial tariff if only this political obstacle to the favourable reception of their tea in America might be removed. The ministers hoped that more tea sold in America would provide a larger American revenue, and they would not give up the remaining token of parliamentary authority over the colonies. Not only did they fail to appreciate the degree to which this attempt to undermine principle by economic inducement affronted men of deep conviction among the colonists. They failed also to see that the concession of the right to the Company to establish a monopoly in the sale of tea in the hands of a few agents would offend important mercantile interests. Nor did they properly weigh the consequences of the discontent which would be aroused by the prospect, which they welcomed, of driving out of business the many merchants who dealt in smuggled tea. In all the chief American ports the Act drove merchants to co-operate with radical politicians in further defiance of British authority. Possibly even British tea shippers may have been moved by jealousy to add to the stream of letters crossing the Atlantic from expatriate colonists and their friends in Britain, denouncing the measure as merely intended to secure a more general submission to the Townshend duty.

In all the major ports steps were taken to prevent the landing of the East India tea and the now familiar methods of intimidation were used or threatened against those who had agreed to act as the Company's agents. In many cases the captains of merchantmen were persuaded to take their consignments back to England. It was the failure to secure this peaceful outcome which led, in the famous 'Boston Tea Party' of 16th December 1773, to the dumping overboard of three shiploads which were about to be landed by the local customs officials. A week later the governor of Massachusetts baldly stated the dilemma which the new Tea Act had posed: 'To enforce the duty appears beyond all comparison more difficult than I ever before imagined. . . . To concede endangers raising the like spirit in other cases of parliamentary authority.'*

This time the ministers felt they could not yield; and the government was in a stronger position than it had been since the eclipse of Chatham. In January 1770 the appointment of Lord North as First Lord of the Treasury in place of Grafton had brought forward into the chief position a popular, and within limits able, minister. Over the past six years the political basis of the government had been broadened by the absorbtion of first one and then another important faction. The death of George Grenville in 1771 removed the most formidable of the opposition leaders and left his followers free to accept a share of places in the administration. During the same period men who shared Chatham's sympathies for the colonists had gradually withdrawn or been edged out of the cabinet, which came to be dominated by convinced imperialists who distrusted the effect of conciliatory policies. The King, too, had become increasingly apprehensive about the attitude of the colonists and was prepared to support a firm policy.

North and his colleagues first explored the possibilities of immediate punitive action under the existing law. But the law officers ruled that insufficient evidence existed to bring

*Historical MSS. Commission, *11th report, appendix, part* V (*Dartmouth MSS.*), p. 344.

particular leaders of the tea riot to trial for treason and that the prerogative of the Crown probably did not cover the closing of the port of Boston and the transfer elsewhere of the custom house. In February the ministers decided that this and other adequate punitive measures must be effected by Act of Parliament. This change of plan greatly broadened and generalized the issues at stake. Mere punitive action under existing law might not necessarily have involved a head-on collision over the constitutional issue of parliamentary supremacy. With the recourse to legislation this became unavoidable.

During the early months of 1774 the ministry brought before Parliament the string of Bills, which became known in the colonies as the 'Coercive' or the 'Intolerable' Acts, and over the enforcement of which the conflict between Great Britain and the colonies finally developed into the revolutionary war.

The first of these measures was purely punitive. The Boston Port Act sanctioned the removal of the custom house to Salem and closed the port to commerce until such time as the inhabitants should have recompensed the East India Company for the lost tea. The navy was to enforce the closure, and it was thought that economic pressure would soon make the populace capitulate. The Act also provided for the seat of the provincial government to be transferred to Salem and for the American Board of Customs also to move there from Boston. The Bill met little opposition in Parliament, for the destruction of the tea was generally regarded as a criminal act deserving punishment. Hardly anyone was prepared to condone it, and only a few voices were raised against the indiscriminate penalizing of the whole population for the actions of a few.

Graver issues were raised by the Massachusetts Bay Regulating Act. It was intended to reinforce the royal executive in the colony. The elected council enjoyed by the province under the terms of its charter was to be replaced by one nominated by the Crown, of the type usual in the royal governments. By this means the governor would be strengthened both in his executive capacity and in his dealings with the legislature of which the council formed part. The assembly was to be deprived of powers it had enjoyed, or usurped, over the appointment and direction of local officials: the governor was vested with full power to appoint and dismiss all inferior officers of the law, including the subordinate judges and the sheriffs. The executive was given greater weight in the appointment of juries: these were to be summoned by the county sheriffs instead of being selected by the freeholders. Town meetings, in which New England democracy had found vigorous expression, and which in Boston provided a constant vehicle for the resistance movement, were placed under severe restraint. The Act limited town meetings to one a year and restricted their function to purely local matters – the election of officers and the passing of local by-laws. A special meeting might only be called by permission of the governor.

Such a statutory alteration of the Massachusetts charter and the provincial constitution amounted to a further deliberate affirmation of the supreme power of Parliament within the empire, one which had the most serious implications for all the colonies. Should it stand, they could claim no constitutional rights but those Parliament might see fit to concede to them. Such a restraint was intolerable to the strong self-reliant communities on the American mainland. It is probable that the Boston Port Act alone would have caused the other mainland colonies to rally round Massachusetts: the Regulating Act put it beyond doubt that they would do so.

Two other statutes were intended to provide for the better security of law and order in Massachusetts. An Administration of Justice Act laid down that persons accused of capital offences as a consequence of carrying out their duties, might, at the discretion of the governor, be sent for trial to some other colony or to Great Britain. Regarding this as an encouragement to soldiers to use violence, the Bostonians in due course dubbed it a 'murder bill'. A Quartering Act gave the governor enlarged and defined powers to quarter troops in uninhabited houses, barns, and outhouses, and if necessary, in private dwellings, in areas suitably located for the performance of their duties. This measure overrode the colonial contention, that troops should be quartered only in barracks – which meant, so far as concerned Boston, that they would have been stationed away from the town in the island fort of Castle William.

In Parliament all these enactments, except the Boston Port Act, were strenuously opposed by the Rockingham Party and by the followers of Chatham. In a debate on yet another proposal for the repeal of the tea duty Edmund Burke put the

American case squarely in the perspective of history and of constitutional principle:

> The feelings of the colonies were formerly the feelings of Great Britain. Their's were formerly the feeling of Mr. Hampden when called upon for the payment of 20s. Would 20s. have ruined Mr. Hampden's fortune? No! but the payment of half 20s. on the principle it was demanded would have made him a slave. It is the weight of that preamble, of which you are so fond, and not the weight of the duty, that the Americans are unable and unwilling to bear.

But, as he afterwards wrote, parliamentary opinion was overwhelmingly on the government side, 'from a general notion, that *some* act of power was become necessary; and that the hands of government ought to be strengthened, by affording an entire credit to the opinions of ministry. . . . The popular current', Burke added, in this report to the New York Assembly on the Port Bill, 'both within doors and without, at present sets strongly against America.'* 'It is not', declared another member of the opposition, 'an error of the ministry, it is an error of the nation: I see it wherever I go. People are of the opinion that these measures ought to be carried into execution.' In the debate on the Port Bill Lord North voiced a general apprehension, 'that at Boston we were considered as two independent states; but we were no longer to dispute between legislation and taxation, we were now to consider only whether or not we [had] any authority there.' Time and again during the following weeks this theme was hammered home by ministerial spokesmen, and newspaper comment generally hostile in tone to the Bostonians helped to inflame public as well as parliamentary opinion. The House was with the Prime Minister when he sounded the note of authority: 'Convince your colonies that you are able, and not afraid to control them, and, depend upon it, obedience will be the result of your deliberations.'† The coercive acts, far from being, as Boston patriots and less well-informed British critics averred, the work of a corrupt, unrepresentative clique, were a clear

---

The Parliamentary History, vol. xvii, cols. 1224–25; *The correspondence of Edmund Burke*, vol. ii, *July 1768–June 1774*, ed. by Lucy S. Sutherland (1960), p. 528.

†British Museum, Egerton MSS. 257, fos. 141–42; *The Parliamentary History* vol. xvii, cols. 1166–67, 1273.

expression of national policy, opposed only by small but vehement minority groups. In both Houses of Parliament they were approved by large majorities.

While Parliament sanctioned the policy, the government looked to the means. General Gage, the commander-in-chief in America, was sent back with an additional commission as governor of Massachusetts, and relief troops originally intended for other destinations were diverted to Boston. Civil and military power was now to be used hand in hand for the enforcement of that submission which British statesmen felt to be essential to the survival of the Empire. To Gage the colonial secretary wrote in June: 'The constitutional authority of the Kingdom over its colonies must be vindicated, and its laws obeyed throughout the whole Empire. . . . its very existence depends on the present moment. . . . destruction must follow disunion.'*

During this same session of Parliament the North ministry also secured the enactment of another important colonial measure, the Quebec Act. This formed no part of the punitive legislation, though it soon came to be represented as such by the colonists. One scholar has recently pointed out that, 'the ministry seems never to have discussed its Canadian policies in Cabinet at the same time as it considered the problem of the American colonies.'† Although the concurrent American crisis may to some extent have influenced the timing and the provisions of the Act, the principles behind it had long been under consideration. It was intended to deal with unsolved problems of civil government, both in the French-speaking colony in the St. Lawrence valley, and also in the wilderness between the great lakes and the Ohio, where a thin scattering of French squatters and *voyageurs* had hitherto been left without any civil government at all.

Under the royal proclamation of 1763 the former French colony of Quebec, limited to the St. Lawrence valley, had been provided, in anticipation of a rapid influx of British settlers, with a system of representative government on the usual colonial pattern. This proved unworkable, for few British took up residence, and the operation of the Test Acts debarred the

---

*Cited in B. Donoughue, *British Politics and the American Revolution, 1773–75* (1964), p. 167.
†*Ibid.*, p. 108.

Roman Catholic population from public life. The Catholic church and French civil law also presented problems requiring special regulation. The circumstances had in fact made it impossible for the governor and his staff to implement their instructions, and the Quebec Act, to a large degree, merely regularized the arrangements which, regardless of the proclamation, had been dictated by necessity for the peace and good government of the colony. Legislation was to be by the governor and a nominated legislative council. The Test Acts were made inoperative within the province and Catholics were admitted to public office. Full recognition was given to the Roman Catholic church establishment, including its right to the collection of tithes from its communicants. The introduction of British criminal law was confirmed, but French civil law, including the law of property, was to have full force. These provisions provided a tolerable framework of government for a population of alien tradition without experience of representative government, hitherto excluded from public life and enjoying the customary regulation of its religious and civil affairs only on sufferance.

At the same time the jurisdiction of the governor of Quebec was extended into the interior north and west of a line extending up the St. Lawrence, through Lake Ontario and along the Niagara river to Lake Erie, along the western edge of Pennsylvania to the Ohio, and thence along the Ohio to the Mississippi. Indian affairs might be brought under some sort of regulation, and at the same time civil government provided for the thinly-scattered population of some 1,500 French-Canadian frontiersmen living among the Indian tribes, whose very existence had in many cases not been known in 1763. This part of the Act was a last and long-delayed attempt to erect some other plan for the control of the wilderness in place of that which had been destroyed through denial of colonial funds by the resistance to the Stamp Act. In the mid-'sixties a proposal by Shelburne for controlled settlements in the interior, coupled with a financial provision to be raised by quit-rents, had been still-born, and for some years the situation on the frontier had gradually been dissolving into anarchy. In 1768 the regulation of trade with the Indians was handed back to the colonies, with the consequence that regulation virtually ceased. In the same year the government sanctioned the establishment of a new line of settlement further west than the Proclamation line of 1763. But this did little to satisfy the insatiable demands of land speculators, or of squatters whose incursions on Indian lands proceeded with increasing momentum as economy dictated the withdrawal of British regulars from the costly posts in the wilderness. In 1771 the crumbling walls of Fort Chartres on the Mississippi were abandoned, and the troops were also withdrawn from Fort Pitt. The Virginians moved in and an Indian war followed. By 1773 a Pennsylvania syndicate was beginning to negotiate purchases of lands from the Indians in the Illinois country.

The fixing of the boundary of Quebec, which placed this area out of bounds to settlement, was primarily an attempt to stabilize the frontier region, reduce the pressure on the Indians and the dangers of consequent frontier warfare, maintain peaceable conditions for the fur-trade carried on along the lakes and the St. Lawrence, and win the loyalty of the French frontiersmen. That the measure also confirmed anew the limitations set upon the westward expansion of some of the older colonies undoubtedly appealed to some of the ministers in the impassioned atmosphere of the spring of 1774. But this was not a primary consideration, and the government specifically allowed the limitation to be provisional and temporary.

The Quebec Act, though in essence a statesmanlike measure intended to deal with quite separate problems, was nevertheless violently resented by the American colonists. In New England, especially, anti-Catholic feeling was virulent – as it still was among the lower ranks of society in Britain. The establishment of a nominated legislature, contemporaneously with the abolition of the elected council in Massachusetts, seemed to them clear evidence of a settled design to whittle away the institutions of representative government in the colonies. The new Quebec boundary appeared a denial of their destiny to expand westward into the unsettled wilderness. As a result of its timing, a measure commendable in itself was plausibly represented by colonial leaders as one more step in the unfolding of a deliberate plan of authoritarian control, incompatible with the liberties of Englishmen, and incompatible with the liberties to which the colonists had long been accustomed and which they regarded as their natural right.

As the British authorities soon discovered, it was one thing

to pass coercive enactments against the colony of Massachusetts: it was quite another to enforce them. In fact it was nearly
a year before a thorough-paced attempt was made to do so,
bringing in its train armed conflict between Great Britain
and the colonies. In the meantime, despite British hesitation,
the very threat explicit in the coercion acts was sufficient to
cause the colonists to take almost every action in defence of
their own claims short of actual war.

When General Gage arrived at Boston in May 1774, with
his governor's commission requiring him to put punitive
legislation into effect, he found it impossible to exercise any
authority in the area outside that immediately commanded
by the guns of the British warships in the harbour. The port
was closed; but punishing the tea rioters or securing compensation for the East India Company – two main points in his
instructions – were out of the question. On his summoning a
new General Court at Salem, the elections produced an assembly and council both pledged to the hilt to support the chartered rights of the colony. When the Court met it defiantly
voted, before Gage could dissolve it, a call for a continental
congress to defend American rights. Samuel Adams and the
Boston radicals began to organize a non-importation covenant
throughout the province and paid no attention to the governor's proclamation against it. Informed by Gage that no further
town meetings were to be held without his consent, the select-
men of Boston blandly told him that they would meet in due
course under the last resolutions for adjournment of the current
meeting and that no application to him was necessary.

In August Gage received the text of the Regulating Act, and,
in preparation for a meeting of the new-style General Court,
he published the names of the thirty-six men who had been
nominated as councillors. Nearly all of them had been consistent supporters of imperial authority during the conflicts of
the past ten years. Immediately a storm of popular fury was
unleashed against them, and threats of personal violence and
the destruction of their property induced most of them to
resign or to take refuge with the governor in Boston. Throughout the province county conventions and town meetings,
assembled contrary to law without the governor's consent,
passed resolutions affirming that 'a free people must have
constitutional checks upon government, and that appointment

of officials at pleasure, destruction of trial by jury, and payment of officials by a power over which the people had no
control, destroyed those constitutional checks'.* The language
used, and the resolutions, at all these meetings echoed the
feeling that the colonists would be justified in appealing to
force to prevent the enforcement of the Coercive Acts. A
subsequent meeting of delegates from the townships voted
the nominated council to be unconstitutional, denied the
supremacy of Parliament, and called for a provincial congress.
In September the famous resolves of the convention of Suffolk
county, in which Boston lay, echoed in the resolutions of other
county meetings, denounced the Coercive Acts as plainly unconstitutional, demanded a commercial boycott of Great
Britain, and recommended military training as a preparation
for the defence of their rights.

Gage regarded it as impossible, with the troops at his
command, to enforce order or obedience to the Coercive Acts.
Having ordered the new General Court to meet at Salem, he
finally did not convene it, being afraid to take to it the councillors who had come to him at Boston for protection. At the
beginning of September he reported despairingly, that the
resistance movement involved not merely the Boston rabble
but the 'freeholders and farmers' of the province – the people
were almost unanimously opposed to the royal government –
and he clamoured for military reinforcements as indispensable
for the restoration of imperial authority. His action in taking
over the provincial supply of gunpowder at Boston produced
an uproar: it was reported that nearly 20,000 armed men from
the countryside began to converge upon the town, and only
with difficulty did the radical leaders persuade them to return
home. Irregular military training proceeded apace, and consignments of arms and gunpowder began to arrive from
Holland and other continental sources. In October, after
Gage had declined to summon the General Court, the townships defied him by sending representatives to a provincial
congress. The members of this body had explicit instructions
from their constituents to oppose any alteration of the colony's
charter. Outside Boston this unauthorized assembly, with the
help of local committees set up to execute its resolutions,

*Cited in R. E. Brown, *Middle-Class Democracy and the Revolution in Massa-
chusetts, 1691–1780* (Ithaca, 1955), p. 345.

became the only effective government within the province.

As the news of successive Coercive Acts spread along the Atlantic seaboard, a massive movement of support for Massachusetts welled up in the other colonies. Through township and county meetings, in defiance of the protests of colonial governors, calls went out for a cessation of trade with Britain and the convening of a continental congress. In face of the attack upon the Massachusetts charter no colony but felt its liberties insecure. Particularly significant was the lead given by Virginia, the 'Old Dominion', perhaps still at this date the most populous of the provinces. Although the governor dissolved the House of Burgesses for its contumacious behaviour, an important group of its members resumed their activities in unofficial session and worked briskly for both objects. The opinions of the more extreme among them found expression in Thomas Jefferson's *Summary View of the Rights of British America*, which denied the authority of Parliament over the colonies and made them out to be as separate, save for the personal union under the sovereign, as Hanover was from Britain, or as Scotland had been from England during the century preceding the Act of Union. Everywhere throughout the colonies local popular organizations sprang into being to secure the election of representatives to a congress and to give them clear instructions about the objects they were to pursue – the vindication of the liberties of Englishmen in America and the adoption of a commercial boycott to bring the British to heel. The following words of Washington stated a conviction echoed frequently in the letters of colonists at this time: 'The crisis is arrived when we must assert our rights or submit to every imposition, that can be heaped upon us, till custom and use shall make us as tame and abject slaves, as the blacks we rule over with such arbitrary sway.'*

Representatives of all the old colonies save Georgia assembled at Philadelphia in early September 1774. In deference to conservative feeling this congress discussed – but in the end rejected – a proposal by Joseph Galloway for a federal structure of government in British North America which would stand in something like a 'dominion relationship' with the Parliament and royal executive at home. Galloway's plan

*The Writings of George Washington, ed. John C. Fitzpatrick, 39 v. (Washington, 1931–44), III, p. 242.

provided for the establishment of an all-American legislature, a Grand Council, composed of members chosen triennially by the legislatures of the different provinces, and of a chief executive, a President General, to hold office during the King's pleasure. These organs were to be subordinate to those in Great Britain but were to have control over all commercial, civil, criminal, and police affairs of general concern to the colonies. A power to veto all legislation by Parliament affecting the colonies would have established the essential constitutional point so far as the colonies were concerned. Concession to the British authorities of a similar power to veto legislation passed by the Grand Council would preserve the constitutional link between the two communities. Even this scheme involved a degree of connection with Great Britain no longer acceptable to the majority of the delegates. Also it cut across the jealously-guarded autonomy of each separate province. Although rejected the plan is however of interest, both as a reflection of what was thought possible by more conservative delegates, and because it foreshadowed other plans for union in America.

Having set aside Galloway's proposal, the congress decided during October to stand by Massachusetts and defy the Coercive Acts. It adopted a declaration of rights, passed resolutions for a petition to George III, and made declarations encouraging resistance by the separate colonial legislatures. The declaration of rights rehearsed the doctrine, that as Americans could not, from the circumstances, be represented in Parliament, their own assemblies must and did hold full powers of legislation in all matters of domestic concern. The delegates accepted in principle the traditional restrictions of the trade and navigation acts (though they declared that parliamentary regulation was subject to consent and not a matter of right), but they regarded as grievances which must be redressed all legislation concerning trade and taxation passed since the Sugar Act of 1764; and as a matter of course, they demanded the repeal of the Quebec Act and the Coercive Acts, which in their eyes were utterly unconstitutional. Their petition to George III sought in respectful terms redress of all grievances listed in the declaration and animadverted against the ministers who had given him evil advice on American measures. Finally the delegates passed resolutions decreeing a commercial boycott and signed a bond of association committing their respective colonies to a strict non-importation, non-exportation, and non-consumption agreement.

In the wake of the congress the colonists girded themselves vigorously for the defence of their rights. Everywhere loyalists were hounded down and royal officials rendered powerless. The fabric of royal colonial government dissolved, as everywhere committees of association assumed executive powers, and local conventions and congresses took over the role of the colonial legislatures. In December the governor of Virginia reported:*

> The associations . . . recommended by the people of this colony, and adopted by what is called the continental congress, are now enforcing throughout this country with the greatest rigor. A committee has been chosen in every county, whose business it is to carry the association of the congress into execution; which committee assumes an authority to inspect the books, invoices, and all the secrets of the trade and correspondence of merchants; to watch the conduct of every inhabitant without distinction; and to send for all such as come under their suspicion, into their presence, to interrogate them . . . and to stigmatize, as they term it, such as they find transgressing what they are hardy enough to call the laws of the congress; which stigmatizing, is no other than inviting the vengeance of an outrageous and lawless mob. . . .

Every township, he added, was arming a company to protect its committee, magistrates declined to act save as committeemen, and the lawyers had withdrawn from the superior court of the province. As the year ended revolutionary committees were active almost everywhere, encouraging drilling, organizing the seizure of military stores in government establishments, setting up manufactories of gunpowder, and arranging the purchase abroad of arms and munitions. The gage thrown down so resolutely by Lord North's ministry had been taken up with no less determination in America.

* *The Parliamentary History*, xviii, col. 314.

CHAPTER SIX

The End of an Empire, 1775-1783

By the beginning of 1775 the stands respectively taken by the British government and by the colonial leaders pointed inexorably to armed conflict. Only a substantial surrender by one side or the other could avert it. Neither was inclined to such a step. In the eyes of the colonists, to give way to acts of power would be an abdication of their status as free men. In a letter of October 1774, which doubtless reflected the past weeks of earnest, passionate discussion at Williamsburg and Philadelphia, Washington rebuked an old military associate, now likely soon to be found on the opposing side.*

You reason from effects, not causes; otherwise you would not wonder at a people who are every day receiving fresh proofs of a systematic assertion of an arbitrary power, deeply planned to overturn the laws and constitution of their country, and to violate the most essential and valuable rights of mankind, being irritated and with difficulty restrained from acts of the greatest violence and intemperance.... It is not the wish or interest of that government [Massachusetts] or any other upon this continent, separately or collectively, to set up for independency; but this you may at the same time rely on, that none of them will ever submit to the loss of those valuable rights and privileges which are essential to the happiness of every free State, and without which life, liberty and property are rendered totally insecure.

Not even a return to the relatively harmonious working system of the Walpolean era would now satisfy the colonists. The definition of claims by the British government during the last twelve years had provoked opposing definitions in America, and it was clear that only on a basis of total legislative independence in domestic matters would the relationship with Great Britain now be tolerable.

On the other hand, by the end of 1774, the British govern-

* *The Writings of George Washington*, ed. John C. Fitzpatrick, 39 v. (Washington, 1931–44), III, pp. 385–86.

ment was obdurately convinced of and committed to the view, that a dominant minority in the colonies was aiming at independence, and that either British authority must be reasserted in the colonies (at this stage, more particularly in Massachusetts), or else the whole fabric of empire would dissolve and Britain sink back into the role of a minor power. Faced with such an apparent catastrophe they were prepared to risk civil war within the Empire – would indeed have already run the risk and reaped its consequences had there been sufficient troops in Boston for Gage to attempt to follow his instructions. Early in 1775, as soon as Parliament met, extra troops and naval forces were voted, and reinforcements were dispatched to Boston. The New England provinces were proclaimed to be in a state of rebellion, and an Act was passed restraining them from all trade and from participation in the Newfoundland fisheries until submission was made. As one province after another made known its sympathy for New England, these restraints were soon afterwards extended to most of the other colonies. In the debates which accompanied these measures, ministers rested their case almost exclusively on the need to secure a clear admission of subordination from the colonies. They brushed aside opposition warnings, that the colonists, in resisting parliamentary taxation, were united on firm constitutional ground, and that to exact submission by military force was impracticable. In their eyes the willingness expressed by the Continental Congress to abide by the commercial restraints in existence before 1763 was insufficient. Before any concessions were made, Parliament's authority must be acknowledged and the relief claimed by the colonies sought as a matter of grace, not as a matter of right. If this surrender were made there would, ministers hinted, be generous treatment of grievances, including the abandonment of parliamentary taxation. Early in February, in a general debate on the American situation, North declared: 'He did not mean to tax America . . . if they would submit, and leave to us the constitutional right of supremacy, the quarrel would be at an end.'* In the Commons majorities phenomenal by eighteenth-century standards supported the ministers' policy, the government vote often approaching, occasionally exceeding, 300, well over half the total membership of the House.

* *The Parliamentary History*, xviii, cols. 264–5.

A fortnight later North presented 'conciliatory propositions' to the Commons, and he revealed the extreme limit of
concession which the ministers were prepared to make until
after they had experienced military defeat. The substance of
these proposals was that, provided the colonists would make
sufficient and permanent provision for the support of their
civil government and the administration of justice, and for
defence, and in time of war contribute extraordinary supplies
in a reasonable proportion to what was raised in Great Britain,
then – for so long and no longer – there would be no resort to
parliamentary taxation. Parliament would still exercise the
power of controlling trade, but the yield of any taxation
incidental to such legislation would be paid into the treasury
of the colony concerned; and any representation from any
colony proposing changes in the commercial regulations would
be given full consideration. Action would be taken to put the
propositions into effect as soon as acceptable proposals were
received from any colony.*

North's propositions had the apparent merit of placing the
colonists in a position of taxing themselves if they accepted
the accompanying conditions. The principle of 'no taxation
without representation' would thus seem to be conceded. Some
of the more conservative colonial leaders were inclined to
believe that this concession was all that was necessary and
wished to explore the possibilities of conciliation on this
ground. But at bottom the proposals were entirely unacceptable to American opinion. In reality they represented much
less of a concession than the legislation of 1766 – for if the
colonies were to make ample, permanent provision for all
governmental services, they would lose that financial control
over the executive which they had gradually built up during
the century and which they now correctly regarded as one
essential feature of a free political society. The provincial
executives would be left free to act as the agents of the imperial
government: central control would increase and local autonomy be further eroded. And the concession of 'no taxation
without representation' was quite illusory. The colonists would
tax themselves under threat and without being left any discretion. As one parliamentary critic pointed out, the proposals
amounted to the threat: 'Give me as much as I wish, till I

Ibid. col. 319–22.

say enough, or I will take it from you.'* All the signs pointed
to a demand for greater exactions than had been attempted by
the retention of the tea duty in 1770. In America the implications were fully realized. The Virginia House of Burgesses
commented:†

> The British government has no right to intermeddle with the
> support of civil government in the colonies. For us, not for them, has
> government been instituted here. . . . We cannot conceive that any
> other legislature has a right to prescribe either the number or pecu-
> niary appointment of our officers. . . . We have a right to give our
> money as the Parliament does theirs, without coercion. . . . It is not
> merely the mode of raising, but the freedom of granting our money
> for which we have contended, without which we possess no check on
> the royal prerogative.

North's propositions were a manoeuvre, not a concession; and
as a manoeuvre they failed. They conceded none of the substance demanded by colonial opinion and they failed entirely
to drive a wedge between New England and the other colonies.
Only in Parliament did the government gain. Some of the
independents were satisfied that a gesture of conciliation had
been made; and a number of members, by vehemently denouncing the ministers for yielding too much, confirmed the
acceptability of a firm policy towards the colonies.

In the early months of 1775 Chatham and Burke both
offered proposals for conciliation with the colonies.

Chatham's Conciliation Bill started from a premise which
by now had been overtaken by events. It recited that the
colonies 'have been, are, and of right ought to be dependent
upon the imperial crown of Great Britain, and subordinate
unto the British Parliament'. It affirmed Parliament's right
to control trade and the Crown's right to make troop dispositions in the colonies at its discretion. Chatham offered a
number of specific concessions which would have met certain
particular colonial grievances: recognition of and negotia-
tion through congress, and its erection into a permanent
imperial institution; renunciation of any use of the military
against the liberties of the Americans; statutory abandonment
of any claim to taxing power; assurances of the inviolability

---

Ibid. col. 350 (Hartley).

†Cited, T. J. Wertenbaker, *Give me Liberty. The struggle for self-government
in Virginia* (Phil., 1958).

of colonial charters and constitutions save in case of legal
forfeiture; abrogation of all Acts which interfered with trial
by jury in the colonies and the appointment of judges 'during
good behaviour', as in Britain; and suspension of all other
statutes passed since 1764 against which there was complaint,
to be followed by their repeal when congress had made formal
recognition of the supremacy of Parliament. But although
Chatham stressed the theoretical sole power of the colonial
assemblies to impose taxation upon the colonists, no more than
the ministers was he prepared to capitulate completely on the
financial issue, and his plan envisaged a grant of a permanent
revenue by the colonists which would be at the disposal not of
their own assemblies but of Parliament.* In the tense atmosphere of 1775 there was little chance of the colonists complying
with this condition; in any case, majority opinion in Parliament
was dead against concession.

Burke's proposals, offered in the Commons a few weeks later,
came nearer to providing ground for conciliation, but by 1775
they were probably unacceptable to the colonists, as they
certainly were to the majority in Parliament.† Believing that
the government should come to terms with realities and acknowledge both the material power and the intellectual premises of the colonists, Burke argued that an empire was an
aggregate of many states under one common head, in which
the subordinate parts had extensive local privileges and immunities. The line between these privileges and the supreme
authority might be impossible to draw, and frequently there
would be disputes as to where it lay. But in such instances –
and specifically in the case of taxation then at issue – the only
satisfactory solution was to achieve compromises acceptable
in practice to all the parties concerned and to avoid insistence
on questions of right. The real issue, Burke declared was,
'not whether you have a right to render your people miser-
able; but whether it is not your interest to make them happy.
It is not what a lawyer tells me I *may* do; but what humanity,
reason, and justice tell me I ought to do.' He rightly insisted,
that the ordinary commercial intercourse between Britain
and the colonies fostered by self-interest was worth far more to
Britain than any advantage that might be grudgingly obtained

* *The Parliamentary History*, xviii, cols. 198–204.
† *Ibid.* cols. 478–538.

by the assertion of supreme authority. Any financial contribution to imperial expenditure should be obtained on a voluntary
basis as before 1763. Questions of right should be buried in
oblivion. In this spirit he proposed the resolution: 'That it
hath been found by experience, that the manner of granting
the said supplies and aids, by the said general assemblies, hath
been more agreeable to the inhabitants of the said colonies,
and more beneficial and conductive to the public service,
than the mode of giving and granting aids and subsidies in
parliament to be raised and paid in the said colonies.' With
that rare imaginative grasp which, though not in itself alone
constituting high statesmanship, is yet an essential part of it,
he drew forth for his hearers the impalpable essence of inter-
imperial co-operation: 'the close affection which grows from
common names, from kindred blood, from similar privileges,
and equal protection . . . ties which though light as air, are as
strong as links of iron'. As an essential preliminary to recon-
ciliation Burke, like Chatham, advocated the repeal of all
legislation passed since 1763 which was disagreeable to the
colonists.

Burke's plan conceded virtually everything demanded by
the first Continental Congress. It did not merely put the clock
back to 1763: it allowed also for the dynamic growth inherent
in any healthy political system. Even a drift from dependence
to voluntary partnership was compatible with its terms – an
outcome Burke himself in 1775 was prepared to contemplate,
though he did not think it imminent. Such a vision was far
above the heads of the generality of British politicians. After
1773 the greater part of the British political nation had become
convinced that a breach within the empire was likely, that it
was consciously intended by an aggressive, dominant minority
of colonial leaders, that only through the use of force might it
still be prevented, and that failure to prevent it would spell
the end of British prosperity and greatness.

The bitter fruits of these convictions were soon to be reaped.
Within a month the revolutionary war had begun in Massachusetts. In mid-April Governor Gage at Boston received
specific instructions to put down the rebellion in the colony.
The essential stroke – arrest of the leaders of the provincial
congress – was beyond his resources; but he decided to seize
the main dump of rebel supplies in the village of Concord some

sixteen miles away. On the outward march the British troops came into conflict with a small party of American militia at Lexington. Which side fired first is not certain; but the affair set Massachusetts aflame. The British column carried out its operations at Concord, but it was severely harassed and suffered heavy losses on its homeward march; and immediately an army of Massachusetts militia swarmed to the siege of Boston.

The response from leaders in other colonies was swift. Three weeks later, on 10th May 1775, in accordance with arrangements made the previous year, the second Continental Congress assembled at Philadelphia. In face of the outbreak of hostilities in Massachusetts, it quickly assumed the role of a revolutionary government bent on preparations for war. These were pressed forward with vigour in all the colonies. By early March 1776 the Americans were able to force a British withdrawal from Boston and had undertaken a partially successful invasion of Canada which gave them possession for some time of Montreal. Meanwhile British preparations for large-scale war were pushed forward strenuously during the winter of 1775–76, large numbers of troops were recruited, and others were obtained by subsidy treaties with various West German princes.

As a war situation developed, colonial sentiment moved in favour of independence. By the summer of 1776 British administration had everywhere been replaced by *ad hoc* provincial governments. In April Congress declared American ports open to all countries except Britain and advised the separate provinces to maintain or set up governments independent of imperial authority. On 4th July it adopted the momentous resolution, that the colonies be declared independent. In measured language Thomas Jefferson, the chief draftsman of the Declaration, re-stated the Lockian theory of political association, the philosophical ground on which the Americans rested their case:

We hold these truths to be self evident, that all men are created equal, that they are endowed by their Creator with certain unalienable rights, that among these are life, liberty, and the pursuit of happiness. That to secure these rights, governments are instituted among men, deriving their just powers from the consent of the governed. That whenever any form of government becomes destructive of these ends, it is the right of the people to alter or abolish it, and to institute new government, laying its foundation on such principles and organizing its powers in such form, as to them shall seem most likely to effect their safety and happiness.

In twenty-seven brief and cogent sentences the Declaration listed the 'injuries and usurpations' inflicted upon Americans by the British Crown since the accession of George III, from the Revenue Act of 1764 to the recent coercive measures, and rolled towards its momentous conclusion:

We, therefore, the Representatives of the United States of America, in General Congress assembled, appealing to the Supreme Judge of the world for the rectitude of our intentions, do, in the name, and by authority of the good people of these colonies, solemnly publish and declare, that these United Colonies are, and of right ought to be Free and Independent States; that they are absolved from all allegiance to the British Crown, and that all political connection between them and the State of Great Britain is and ought to be totally dissolved. . . . And for the support of this declaration, with a firm reliance on the protection of Divine Providence, we mutually pledge to each other our lives, our fortunes, and our sacred honour.

For some at least of the men who made the decision, it was no easy one. Only after prolonged bitter disappointment, grief, and agony of spirit, did they feel compelled, in face of British obstinacy, to secede from the British community, of which they felt themselves in many ways so much a part. In October 1775 John Adams wrote to his wife:

I saw from the beginning that the controversy was of such a nature that it never would be settled. . . . This has been the source of all the disquietude of my life. . . . The thought that we might be driven to the sad necessity of breaking our connection with Great Britain, exclusive of the carnage and destruction, which it was easy to see must attend the separation, always gave me a great deal of grief.

Much of what had made life worth living he would cheerfully give up to obtain peace and liberty: 'But all these must go and my life too, before I can surrender the right of my country to a free constitution.'* In similar vein Thomas Jefferson wrote:†

*Familiar Letters of John Adams and his wife . . . during the Revolution, ed. Charles Francis Adams (N.Y., 1876), p. 11.

†Marie Kimball, Jefferson. The Road to Glory, 1743–1776 (N.Y., 1943), pp. 271–72.

I am sincerely one of those, too, who would rather be in dependence on Great Britain, properly limited, than on any other nation on earth, or than on no nation. But I am one of those, too, who, rather than submit to the rights of legislating for us, assumed by the British parliament, and which late experience has shown they will so cruelly exercise, would lend my hand to sink the whole Island in the sea.

Only the briefest account can here be given of the war, at the end of which the intentions of the Declaration of Independence were in fact secured.

The first serious British effort to recover control of the colonies did not take effect till mid-1776. At the same time as Congress was moving towards acceptance of the Declaration, substantial British forces were on their way across the Atlantic, and the first major blow was an occupation of New York in July by forces which before long totalled over 30,000 men. The securing of this great port and centre of loyalism was intended to be the prelude to the reduction of the New England provinces, but nothing further was accomplished this year except the occupation of Rhode Island. A small detachment found it impossible to raise effective loyalist support in the southern colonies. An attempted invasion of New England from Canada also came to a halt.

1777 was a year of decision, for it ended in a great American victory at Saratoga, the effects of which were in the long term conclusive. The British plan was for a substantial force to strike south from Canada under General Burgoyne, in order, by securing Albany in upper New York, to prepare the way for severing communications between New England and the other colonies. Had this operation been coordinated with a thrust up the Hudson by the army under General Howe at New York, the chances of a decisive British success would have been great. For the Americans control of the Hudson heights south of Albany was crucial. To defend this position their Continental army commanded by Washington might well have been drawn into a pitched battle in which its inferiority in numbers, arms, and training, and the lack of expertise of its officers from the commander downwards might have proved fatal. A coordinated push could hardly have failed to win the Hudson heights and draw a military cordon round New England. But the need for close coordination was not realized by any of the British ministers or commanding generals. The resistance Burgoyne was likely to encounter was grossly under-estimated: it was thought he could reach and hold Albany without assistance. Howe at New York therefore saw no reason to defer his own pet scheme for the occupation of Philadelphia, and made matters worse by abandoning plans for a direct thrust through New Jersey in favour of a seaborne expedition which kept his army inoperative at sea and then isolated in southern Pennsylvania for many critical weeks. In consequence, although during 1777 the British secured control of Philadelphia and parts of New Jersey, Pennsylvania and Delaware, they suffered a crushing loss by the destruction of Burgoyne's army at the hands of a numerically superior force of Continental troops and New England militia.*

Saratoga drove the ministry into offering real concessions, of a kind which, four years earlier, might have averted rebellion. The Tea Act and the Massachusetts Charter Act were repealed; by a declaratory Act Parliament renounced the use of its power to tax the colonies; a peace commission was appointed and a contingent repeal of the Prohibitory Act was enacted. The commissioners were empowered to offer if necessary all, and more than all, that had been demanded by the first Continental Congress, provided the Americans would return to their allegiance and accept parliamentary control of imperial trade. They were instructed to salvage what elements of British authority they could, but any terms short of independence might be accepted.

This offer came too late. Congress insisted upon independence – for by their victory they had secured a French alliance. Since 1763 the attention of French statesmen had been focused upon opportunities to restore French prestige and to pull down Great Britain from the position of ascendancy she had won at the Peace of Paris. They shared the British view, that the loss of the colonies would materially reduce British power, and with this purpose in view, starting early in 1776, an increasing measure of clandestine aid flowed across the Atlantic. Spain, allied to France by the Family Compact, followed suit.

*Important contributions to a reassessment of the reasons and responsibility for this British disaster are contained in G. S. Brown, *The American Secretary. The Colonial Policy of Lord George Germain, 1775–1778* (Ann Arbor, Mich. 1963); Piers Mackesy, *The War for America, 1775–1783* (1964); and W. B. Willcox, *Portrait of a General. Sir Henry Clinton in the War of Independence* (N.Y., 1964).

French supplies of arms and gunpowder were a vital factor in sustaining American resistance. After Saratoga France threw off the mask, entered into treaty relations with the United States, and accepted war with Britain as the inevitable consequence. A year later the Spanish, too, entered the conflict, with the recovery of Gibraltar as their major aim. No diplomatic counter-stroke was open to the British government. British diplomatic isolation was a natural and inescapable situation in the 1770s. So long as France was not pressing upon the Low Countries and Germany, Britain had no natural allies on the Continent. France was in a perfect position for once, with no enemy on the Rhine. It was a position which her minister, Vergennes, was careful to maintain. He evaded current German entanglements, and he sought to make it plain, that France had no desire to destroy British power completely and face Europe with a new Bourbon ascendancy; the balance of power in Europe was not to be altered, but Britain was to have her wings clipped by the loss of her colonies.

The immediate American gain from the French alliance was the recovery of Philadelphia and Rhode Island: the British withdrew from both in order to find troops to counter the French threat in the West Indies, and also launched a probe into Georgia which achieved considerable success. The long-term gain lay in the eventual military support, which arrived in 1780, and in the strain placed on the British navy. British naval strength was stretched still further when a third maritime power was drawn into the alliance against her. A vital British concern was the interception of Baltic naval stores and other war supplies shipped to her enemies in neutral bottoms. Most of this neutral carrying trade was in Dutch hands. In 1780 the Empress Catherine of Russia formed an association of Baltic powers, known as the 'Armed Neutrality', to protect neutral shipping rights. The merchant fleets of its members were of little importance. But if the Dutch secured its protection, British pressure on her foes would be seriously checked, and at the end of the year, to forestall this event, the British government declared war on a set of trumped-up charges against the United Provinces. All these developments meant that, from 1778 onwards, for critical periods, the British lost naval control in American waters, in the end with decisive effects.

During 1778 and 1779 both Britain and France were concerned mainly with the campaigns in the West Indies. Although the pressure on the Americans was relieved, they received little direct support from their French allies. But to the British the West Indies was merely a diversion, and as soon as possible they redirected their efforts to the American continent. In 1780 the war of independence momentarily took a new turn with the British capture of Charleston and the apparent subjugation of most of South Carolina as well as Georgia. It was a deceptive triumph, however, for American guerilla operations were sustained by help from the north, and the general left in command, Earl Cornwallis, found it impossible to ease the situation by any effective blow to the northward. In 1781 he attempted to secure control of North Carolina and Virginia. At the critical moment a French fleet moved into the Chesapeake cutting his communications with New York. At Yorktown his troops were hemmed in against the York River by a superior French and American force under Washington without hope of reinforcement or relief, and by his capitulation the last British army available for offensive operations in America was lost. The blow was decisive. Within a few months a majority of members of parliament had become convinced that the recovery of the colonies by force was impossible, the King, despite his stubborn resolution against yielding, had to give way, and a new ministry composed of leaders of the opposition to the war took office, pledged to secure peace, if necessary by the recognition of American independence. Peace on this basis was negotiated during the autumn of 1782, early in the next year hostilities were suspended by a general armistice, and on 3rd September 1783 were signed the definitive treaties which formally signalized the separation of the independent United States from the British Empire.

The British had lost. But competent historians have expressed the view that in the early stages at least they might have won.* In 1775 there was still a great fund of loyal feeling in the colonies. In America the war of independence was a real civil war: many thousands of loyalists served George III in militia units, provincial regiments, or as recruits in the

*See Piers Mackesy, pp. 510 seq., and the very full analysis in E. Robson, *The American Revolution, 1763-1783* (1955), chapters V, VI, and VII.

regular army, and fought with a fratricidal fury rarely shown by the British and German regulars. The seizure of New York in 1776 gave the British the important strategic advantage of interior lines of communication, by land or by sea, all round the crucial arc between Boston and the Virginia tidewater. During the next eighteen months errors of execution rather than an utter lack of resources for the task were the main reasons for defeat. The two most fatal were, first, the failure to pursue a sound and vigorous strategy which would force Washington and the Continental army into pitched battle on unfavourable terms in which they would be destroyed or else be reduced to complete impotence; and second, the failure to take only ground that could be held and to hold ground once taken, for the consequence was the sacrifice of the loyalists in one province after another to rebel vengeance, the destruction of their power such as it was (it was never so great as the government believed), and, more important, the demonstration to the wavering, uncommitted section of the population that it was better to go along with the rebels. Had military skill and boldness gained major successes quickly in the middle colonies, where loyalists were numerous, it is possible that the heart might have gone out of the rebellion: unless this happened, there was little chance of any regular army the British could produce overcoming the *levée en masse* which would otherwise have met it in New England. But the possibility was never tested. The ministers at home failed to understand the urgency, mainly because they consistently underestimated the extent of rebel sentiment and overestimated the strength of the loyalists. And even had they grasped it, the senior British military commanders were not the men to respond. In fighting spirit they were far inferior to the American officers who opposed them. The consequences of mismanagement were fatal. British and loyalist morale gradually fell while that of the rebels rose. Failure to control a large enough area from which food and other essential requirements could be obtained meant that enormous effort had to be diverted into supplying the British forces from England and Ireland, and by 1782 the war must have ground to a halt in any event, for the country's shipping resources were stretched beyond the limit.*

*This last point emerges clearly from a study of this shipping problem by Mr. D. Syrett, to whom I am grateful for this information.

Even had the British won the war in America the political problem would have remained acute. A settlement on British terms would have left unsatisfied deep-seated American aspirations, further sharpened as these would have been by the struggle. And even if the situation could have been kept under control for the time being, for how long would this have been possible? The population of the colonies was doubling itself about every thirty years – a far higher rate of increase than that in the mother country. There were no population-statistics in the eighteenth century, but the general trend was clearly recognized. The significance of this dynamic aspect of the colonial problem appears entirely to have escaped the attention of the ministers. Time and again they said in effect: 'We must assert British authority now, or it will be too late.' But they failed to face the problem, how this authority was to be maintained under foreseeable future conditions. The object for which they led their country into war was, in the long run, incapable of fulfilment. Herein lay an ultimate proof of their lack of statesmanship.

CHAPTER SEVEN

Conclusion

IN the Declaration of Independence the Americans pinned their accusations upon the head of state legally responsible, their renounced sovereign, George III. At home, in the opposition battle in Parliament against North's ministry, Burke and others levelled charges against the all-pervasive influence of a reactionary clique about the King, which manipulated a corrupt parliament to serve its sinister ends in both America and Britain. From both these sources the simple, black and white picture of a defence of liberty against a tyrannical king and his myrmidons entered the folklore of the Revolution and thence, during the following century, passed into some of the writings of British and American historians.

Although the ghost of the old folklore still peers forth occasionally in historical writing, closer investigation has long since stripped it of its credibility. The Declaration of Independence was a manifesto, not an historical account: the passions of the time vibrate through its text. The allegations of the opposition in the British Parliament were but the current cant of politics, often sincerely believed yet clearly contradicted by other words and actions of its propagators, and fully disproved by the work of scholars who have studied the nature of the eighteenth-century British political system. Before the end of the nineteenth century, a generally accepted account of the American Revolution was emerging, in which it was seen as the outcome of a complex and intractable problem of imperial relations.

By the mid-eighteenth century some readjustment of the relationship between Great Britain and the American colonies was in due course clearly inevitable. In their early days, as small offshoots of the English community, the colonies naturally remained within the gravitational pull of English power. They could not escape the oceanic extension of European rivalries, and during the seventeenth and the first half of the eighteenth centuries British power was an essential shield for them against her European competitors for empire. A degree of constitutional and economic subordination stemmed naturally from these circumstances, as it did also from the fact that in some instances colonies had been founded with the deliberate intent of bringing commercial advantage to the mother country. From such a status the British West Indian islands could not hope to escape. Area and climate set too narrow limits upon their growth. But it was far otherwise with the mainland colonies, which, in the eighteenth century, and especially after 1763, had almost unlimited prospects of expansion, and were already rich and powerful and conscious of their strength. As British freemen the colonists demanded an equal voice in the control of their destiny, a demand which clashed with current concepts of the nature of empire.

In the early days of this century a strong emphasis came to be placed by historians on the burdensome nature of colonial economic grievances, stemming from British taxation and commercial and currency control. To Carl Becker, 'the more important ground of opposition' to the Stamp Act in New York was 'economic rather than political'. In the view of a more recent exponent of this school, 'economic breakdown in the Mercantile System . . . was the basic reason for the onset of crisis and the outbreak of revolutionary struggle'.* In the last twenty years or so there has been much destructive criticism of this view and a re-focusing of attention upon two themes: the growing self-sufficiency of the colonies and the seriousness of the constitutional dispute between them and the mother country. O. M. Dickerson has trenchantly attacked the view, that the traditional system of commercial regulation cramped and thwarted colonial economic development.† L. H. Gipson has drawn attention to the buoyant, expanding economies of the mainland colonies during the last twenty years before the Revolution, and he has shown how misplaced was much of the apprehension about the economic consequences of British commercial regulation and taxation after 1763. Justified

* Carl Becker, *The History of Political Parties in New York, 1760–1776* (1909), p. 26. Louis M. Hacker, 'Economic and Social Origins of the American Revolution', in *The Causes of the American Revolution*, ed. John C. Wahlke, revised edn. (Boston, [1962]), p. 10.

† *The Navigation Acts and the American Revolution* (Phil., London, 1951).

grievances there were, including perhaps, particularly, the
inconsistent stringency of the control over colonial paper
currencies after 1764. But the indebtedness of the planters in
the southern colonies was due in no small measure to their
own irresponsibility or incompetence (an able man like
Washington avoided such difficulties), and economic problems
were almost irrelevant in what may be called the heartland
of the Revolution, New England. In Massachusetts, the most
important of the New England provinces, within five years of
the Peace of Paris, the balance of trade with Britain was in the
colony's favour, bills of exchange on London standing at par
without even the usual two per cent discount to pay charges.
Moreover, from trade with Spain, Portugal, the West Indies,
and elsewhere, Massachusetts attracted a sufficient quantity
of gold and silver to maintain a specie currency in circulation:
it had a name as 'the silver money colony'. Other indications
of colonial prosperity can be cited. The iron industry, centred
mainly in Pennsylvania, had developed from very small beginnings in the early eighteenth century to such an extent that
by 1775 the colonies were producing more pig iron and bar
iron than Great Britain. Shipbuilding flourished: it has been
estimated, that a merchantman could be built in Massachusetts at half the cost of construction in England, and that in the
last few years before the Revolution about thirty per cent of
the ships engaged in British commerce were American-built,
an appreciable proportion of these having been sold to merchants in Britain. In all colonies the burden of war debts and
taxation after 1763 was much lighter *per capita* than it was in
Britain. It is, then, small wonder, that General Gage, reporting
on resistance to the Stamp Act, observed, 'That the question
is not of the inexpediency of the Stamp Act, or of the inability
of the colonists to pay the tax, but that it is unconstitutional
and contrary to their rights.'* Recent inquiry, too, has correc-
ted the emphasis formerly placed upon the role of the merchants in resisting British authority. At certain times they
were active, and their discontents have a place in the story of
the Revolution. But often the leadership can be traced to

* On colonial prosperity see L. H. Gipson, *The Coming of the Revolution,
1763–1775* (1954), especially chapters 9 and 10. Much other evidence is
scattered through the volumes of his *magnum opus*, *The British Empire before
the American Revolution*.

other groups; and at the end, in some of the middle colonies, the merchants were predominantly loyalist.

The present trend of interpretation, represented by such writers as E. S. Morgan and R. E. Brown, stresses the ideological and constitutional aspects of the conflict. All through the eighteenth century the colonists, cushioned by immense distances from intermeddling by the central government, had been developing a lively sense of their own political self-sufficiency, attaining in their assemblies a high degree of political sophistication, and chiselling away with great success at the remnants of imperial authority represented by the royal governors. By the mid-eighteenth century British control of public law in the colonies through the instruments of royal government had largely broken down. The policy adopted by Grenville and his successors, of strengthening the central authority of the Empire, only brought out into the light a long-simmering constitutional dispute between an imperial parliament which, historically, claimed supremacy in all matters, including taxation, and a group of colonial legislatures which had largely assumed in practice, and soon afterwards explicitly claimed, equality of status with Parliament, with full and exclusive powers to make laws and levy taxation for the inhabitants within their borders. How the colonial claims were to be reconciled with the concept of imperial unity was beyond the imagination of most men in the eighteenth century. When both sides stuck obstinately to their principles a collision followed.

To a significant degree the story of the loss of the American colonies is a story of the misjudgments and the inadequacy of British politicians. But condemnation must fall less upon the ministers responsible for the earlier stages of the crisis than upon those who attempted to force the issue at the end. It may be said in extenuation of George Grenville and his colleagues, that in face of the facts apparent at the end of the French War, there was a real need for imperial reorganization, and there was little reason to suspect the strength of the reaction to it. What had been won in 1763 had to be defended. Both France and Spain had suffered grievous blows, the one losing Canada, the other the Floridas. It seemed beyond doubt that they would

* H. E. Egerton, *The Causes and Character of the American Revolution* (Oxf. 1931), p. 4.

seek revenge, and therefore that adequate defences must be maintained, both by sea and by land. So long as the American colonies were part of the British Empire they could not escape this consequence of European international rivalries. Indian relations formed a part of this defence problem, for it was feared in London, that the French, working from bases in Spanish territory west of the Mississippi, might exploit Indian sympathies in a future war with formidable results, as they had done in 1754. Experience also indicated the need for central direction of defence and of the mobilization of imperial resources. Divisions and jealousies, as well as mere inaction, among the provinces, had made it difficult to call up the full resources of the Empire or to direct them in accordance with general imperial objectives. These same experiences also suggested that, though the colonies might grumble, no serious united opposition was to be expected from them.

In this situation British governments tried, between 1762 and 1765, to work out and apply a coherent policy for the Empire. A unified defence command was set up in America. Major garrisons were established on the vulnerable flanks of the mainland colonies. Indian territory was brought under military control and a plan of conciliating the Indians adopted. As these arrangements entailed a greatly increased expenditure, Grenville sought to raise a contribution directly from the colonies by a combination of direct and indirect taxation. At the same time he undertook an overhaul of the laws of trade, intended to reapportion economic benefits between the various parts of the Empire.

In retrospect it is evident that Grenville's policy was not the right policy at that time. But it was a logical and rational policy, adapted to deal with the contemporary situation as seen from Whitehall, and proceeding from the basic premise, that Great Britain and the colonies comprised one body politic. The fatal flaw was not obvious during the years when the policy was framed: it only became clear in London at the end of 1765. Grenville had failed to understand the need for consent. The psychological pressures at work in the colonies escaped him. After the tremendous victories of the French War the atmosphere was one of overweening confidence. The colonists saw that the danger of encirclement and confinement to the seaboard by the French was ended, that their only serious European competitor in the exploitation of the North American continent had been bundled out, and that a dazzling prospect of westward expansion opened before them. Apparently their need for British succour was over. The danger of a Bourbon war of revenge was one which their minds failed to grasp. At three thousand miles distance they felt only impatience with European entanglements: the genesis of nineteenth-century isolationism was already present. The dynamism of their own political societies pointed to a greater, not less, independence from the mother country. A large measure of this had already been won and they were not prepared to sacrifice it. The British too were overtaken by *hubris* after 1763. Everywhere the theme was expansion, especially in India, and the foundations of the 'Second British Empire' were being laid. William Pitt echoed this pride in British strength in his speech of 1766 against the Stamp Act: 'In a good cause, on a sound bottom, the force of this country can crush America to atoms.' A conscious imperialism sought more, not less, control over its dependencies.

But if a defence can be made for Grenville's policy, little can be made for the actions of Charles Townshend. Grenville had merely misjudged the American circumstances. Townshend wantonly ignored them, after they had been made crystal-clear by the wave of resistance to the Stamp Act. Also Townshend's revenue measures were an incoherent and inconsequent makeshift, arising largely out of his pathological craving for adulation. Burke justly observed in his celebrated speech on American taxation: 'The original plan of the duties, and the mode of executing that plan, both arose singly and solely from a love of our applause. He was truly a child of the House. He never thought, did, or said, anything but with a view to you.' This legislation poisoned Anglo-American relations to a point at which it became excessively difficult for either side, and particularly for the imperial government which had given the provocation, to make a surrender which would allow a peaceful solution to the dispute.

In 1766, with the prompt policy of repeal and conciliation which reduced the tension, the Empire could, in recognizable shape, have survived the Stamp Act crisis. The interminable dispute over authority posed by Townshend's tea duty was fatal to it. A measure petty in itself raised fears in face of which

the Anglo-American bond could not endure: the fears of the
colonists that they would be reduced to the level of slaves; the
fear of the British that by tolerating an imminent secession of
the colonies they would see their country reduced to the status
of a minor power. Both fears were genuine. Both were unfoun-
ded. The British fears were disproved by the event. And had a
less fervent spirit in the colonies enabled the Anglo-American
dialogue about powers and liberties to continue – as Burke
envisaged – at a lower temperature, without violent interrup-
tion, there are good grounds for presuming that the constitutional bond would not have borne heavily – nor, indeed, for
any great length of time unaltered – upon the colonists. British
industrial supremacy (by that time imminent) tended to
extinguish concern with mercantilist regulations. As the
population and wealth of the American colonies rose rapidly
in relation to those of the mother country, the impact of the
colonists upon the dialogue, intellectual and moral, as well as
material, could hardly have failed to have increasing effect.
Changes in the Anglo-American relationship, which were inevitable, could have come about in some other way than they
did, although undoubtedly issues like slavery would have
posed new and difficult problems of adjustment. In the years
before Lexington there were men on both sides who realized
some at least of these things, but the passions aroused by fear,
by short-term interests, and by ideology, swept them aside.
This is not to say that the Revolution was inevitable. The
Revolution was a human tragedy, for which certain men were
responsible, more particularly because, in Great Britain, the
politicians who had the common sense and the vision were out
of power (owing to their own weaknesses and limitations) and
those who were in power lacked the vision. Undisciplined and
independent as the House of Commons was at that time, it
could respond to a wise and statesmanlike lead if this came
from the ministers whom the King had appointed to do his
business. At the critical period no such lead was given. The
consequences remain: 'The evil that men do lives after them.'
What mark would an Anglo-American commonwealth have
made on the world's destiny in the spacious days of the nineteenth century, and after? Assuredly it would have been
great!

Select Bibliography

(All books listed are published in London, unless otherwise stated)

The standard guide to the historical literature of the period is Stanley Pargellis and D. J. Medley, *Bibliography of British History. The eighteenth century, 1714–1789* (Oxford, 1951). There are also full bibliographies in the volumes cited below by L. H. Gipson and J. R. Alden in the *New American Nation Series*. A rather compressed discussion of the historiography of the colonial and revolutionary period of American history is provided in H. Hale Bellot, *American History and American Historians* (1952), and a fuller treatment in Michael Kraus, *The Writing of American History* (Norman, Okl., 1953). The symposium, *The Causes of the American Revolution*, edited by John C. Wahlke (revised edn., Boston [1962]), reflects the diversity of the interpretations still current among historians.

Two good modern standard outlines of British history spanning the period are Dorothy Marshall, *Eighteenth Century England* (1962) and J. Steven Watson, *The Reign of George III, 1760–1815* (Oxford, 1960). R. Pares, *King George III and the Politicians* (Oxford, 1953), is a brilliant survey of the central political machine at work. The political background in Parliament is analysed in detail in Sir Lewis Namier, *The Structure of Politics at the Accession of George III* (2nd edn., 1957) and *England in the Age of the American Revolution* (2nd edn., 1961), in John Brooke, *The Chatham Administration, 1766–1768* (1956) and in Ian R. Christie, *The End of North's Ministry 1780–1782* (1958). Sir Lewis Namier and John Brooke, *The History of Parliament. The House of Commons, 1754–1790* (3 v., 1964), illustrates the general working of the representative system and provides short up-to-date biographies of the British politicians involved in the crisis. The same authors' *Charles Townshend* (1964) makes a significant contribution to an understanding of the Revenue Act of 1767. Much useful information about the manoeuvres of British politicians is brought into focus with the stages of the colonial crisis in C. R. Ritcheson, *British Politics and the American Revolution* (Norman, Okl., 1954), but this study is somewhat summary and stops short at 1778. For an understanding of the attitudes of the politicians in opposition, G. H. Guttridge, *English Whiggism and the American Revolution* (2nd imp. Berkeley and Los Angeles, 1963) is a lucid and in some respects the best guide, but its schematization of British politics is open to challenge – on this, see Ian R. Christie, 'Was there a "New Toryism" in the earlier part of

George III's reign?' *The Journal of British Studies*, V (1965–66), pp. 60–76. The central administration dealing with the colonies is described in Margaret M. Spector, *The American Department of the British Government, 1768–1782* (New York, 1940).

Vincent T. Harlow, *The Founding of the Second British Empire, 1763–1793* (2 v., 1952–64), vol. I, *Discovery and Revolution*, presents the American crisis in the context of the general trends of British commercial and colonial policy. The most comprehensive modern study is Lawrence Henry Gipson, *The British Empire before the American Revolution, 1754–1776* (12 v., New York, 1936–65) – the last two volumes appeared too late to be consulted in the preparation of this book. Though somewhat diffuse, it is full of fascinating information gleaned from an encyclopaedic range of published and unpublished material. The same author's one-volume survey in the *New American Nation Series – The Coming of the Revolution, 1763–1775* (1954), with full bibliography – is compact and close-knit in argument but has been criticized in E. S. Morgan, 'The American Revolution: Revisions in need of revising', *William and Mary Quarterly*, 3rd s., XIV (1957), pp. 3–15, for neglecting the ineptitudes of British politicians and giving too little weight to the constitutional issues involved. Of older works based on more limited material, C. H. Van Tyne, *The Causes of the War of Independence* (Boston and New York, 1922), ranks as a classic, and H. E. Egerton, *The Causes and Character of the American Revolution* (1923, 2nd imp. 1931), is judicious and well-balanced. John C. Miller, *The Origins of the American Revolution* (New York, 1943, new edn. 1959), presents a narrative well enriched from his special interest in propaganda and his ample knowledge of newspapers and pamphlet literature. Curtis P. Nettels, *The Roots of American Civilization* (2nd edn., New York, 1963), is a valuable survey of the colonial background to the Revolution; but it is not concerned with explanations of British policy, perhaps over-emphasizes the economic grievances of the colonists, and in stressing the 'Americanism' of colonial life gives rather less than due weight to the 'Englishness' of the cultured minority which provided the leadership of the Revolution. On the constitutional framework of the old Empire, A. B. Keith, *Constitutional History of the First British Empire* (Oxford, 1930), is standard, and L. W. Labaree, *Royal Government in America* (New Haven, Conn., 1930), is excellent on its rather more specialist field. The criticism of the historic claims of Parliament to supremacy over the colonies in C. A. McIlwain, *The American Revolution* (New York, 1923), is brilliantly refuted in R. L. Schuyler, *Parliament and the British Empire* (New York, 1929).

G. L. Beer, *British Colonial Policy, 1754–1765* (New York, 1907, new imp., 1933) is now outdated but remains a classic exposition of the coherent and reasoned basis of British policy towards the American colonies up to 1765. Bernhard Knollenberg, *Origin of the American Revolution, 1759–1766* (New York, 1960, revised paperback edn., 1961), is concerned with the extent to which British activities caused discontent in the colonies. It provides a valuable wealth of detail but is somewhat undiscriminating in emphasis. The revised edition omits important appendices. The Stamp Act is brilliantly treated in E.S. and Helen M. Morgan, *The Stamp Act Crisis* (Chapel Hill. 1953, revised paperback edn., 1963), and there are also some important recent articles: E. S. Morgan, 'Colonial Ideas of Parliamentary Power', *William and Mary Quarterly*, 3rd s., V (1948), pp. 311–41, and VI (1949), pp. 162–70, and 'The Postponement of the Stamp Act', *ibid.*, VII (1950), pp. 353–92; and C. R. Ritcheson, 'The Preparation of the Stamp Act', *ibid.*, X (1953), pp. 543–59. On the crisis over the colonial tea duty B. W. Labaree, *The Boston Tea Party* (New York, 1964), is excellent, and the British riposte with the Coercive Acts is analysed in detail with much new material in B. Donoughue, *British Politics and the American Revolution. The Path to War, 1773–75* (1964).

Among works on special aspects of the crisis, Jack M. Sosin, *Whitehall and the Wilderness. The Middle West in British Colonial Policy, 1760–1775* (Lincoln, Neb., 1961), adds important material not available at the time of publication of C. W. Alvord, *The Mississippi Valley in British Politics* (2 v., Cleveland, 1917), or T. P. Abernethy, *Western Lands and the American Revolution* (Charlottesville, 1937). Recent studies of the development of Anglo-American tension in relation to colonial constitutional evolution in particular regions or colonies include J. P. Greene, *The Quest for Power. The Lower Houses of Assembly in the Southern Colonies, 1689–1776* (Chapel Hill, 1963); T. J. Wertenbaker, *Give me Liberty. The Struggle for Self-Government in Virginia* (Phil., 1958); and R. E. Brown, *Middle Class Democracy and the Revolution in Massachusetts, 1691–1780* (Ithaca, 1955), which has been criticized for neglecting oligarchical tendencies in Massachusetts politics in David Syrett, 'Town-Meeting Politics in Massachusetts, 1776–1786', *William and Mary Quarterly*, 3rd s., XXI (1964), pp. 353–66. Of value for their discussion of colonial commercial interests are A. M. Schlesinger, *The Colonial Merchants and the American Revolution, 1763–1776* (New York, 1918), and (though sometimes unreliable) O. M. Dickerson, *The Navigation Acts and the American Revolution* (Phil., London, 1951).

A good up-to-date treatment of the war of independence, narrowly defined, is J. R. Alden's perhaps mistitled book, *The American Revolution, 1775–1783* (1954), in the *New American Nation Series*. P. Mackesy, *The War for America, 1775–1783* (1964), treats the struggle in the wider perspective of the European war which developed after 1777 and pays more attention than most works to problems of logistics and war administration. E. Robson, *The American Revolution, 1763–1783* (1955), contains some suggestive but not wholly digested essays. Other leading contributions to an elucidation of British war policy are G. S. Brown, *The American Secretary. The Colonial Policy of Lord George Germain, 1775–1778* (Ann Arbor, 1963), and W. B. Willcox, *Portrait of a General. Sir Henry Clinton in the War of Independence* (New York, 1964). The standard general survey of war diplomacy from the American point of view is S. F. Bemis, *Diplomacy of the American Revolution* (New York, 1935). Expansionist motives in the war policy of the rebel colonists are emphasized in chapters II and III of R. W. Van Alstyne, *The Rising American Empire* (Oxford, 1960). R. B. Morris, *The Peacemakers. The Great Powers and American Independence* (New York, 1965), is an immensely learned and detailed survey. There is nothing comparable for the British side of the war, though Isabel de Madariaga, *Britain, Russia and the Armed Neutrality of 1780. Sir James Harris's Mission to St. Petersburg during the American Revolution* (1962), is excellent and, together with the discussion of the peace negotiations in Harlow (above), goes some way to fill the gap.

Finally, the reader seeking some acquaintance with original material can turn to the selections in *Sources and Documents illustrating the American Revolution, 1764–1788, and the formation of the Federal Constitution*, edited by S. E. Morison (new imp., New York, 1965); *Prologue to Revolution. Sources and Documents on the Stamp Act Crisis, 1764–1766, edited by E. S. Morgan* (Chapel Hill, 1959); and *The Debate on the American Revolution, 1761–1783*, edited by Max Beloff (*The British Political Tradition Series*, 1949). A new series providing a magnificent collection of colonial pamphlet material has begun to appear with *Pamphlets of the American Revolution*, vol. I, *1750–1765* (Camb., Mass., 1965), under the general editorship of Bernard Bailyn. To the immense range of original correspondence listed in the bibliographies mentioned above one important recent addition is *The Correspondence of Edmund Burke* (Camb., 1958, in progress), of which five volumes have so far appeared under the general editorship of T. W. Copeland.

Index